# Participatory Design

# Synthesis Lectures on Human-Centered Informatics

Editor
**John M. Carroll**, *Penn State University*

Human-Centered Informatics (HCI) is the intersection of the cultural, the social, the cognitive, and the aesthetic with computing and information technology. It encompasses a huge range of issues, theories, technologies, designs, tools, environments, and human experiences in knowledge work, recreation and leisure activity, teaching and learning, and the potpourri of everyday life. The series publishes state-of-the-art syntheses, case studies, and tutorials in key areas. It shares the focus of leading international conferences in HCI.

Participatory Design
Susanne Bødker, Christian Dindler, Ole S. Iversen, and Rachel C. Smith

The Trouble With Sharing: Interpersonal Challenges in Peer-to-Peer Exchange
Airi Lampinen

Interface for an App: The Design Rationale Leading to an App that Allows Someone with Type 1 Diabetes to Self-Manage their Condition
Bob Spence

Organizational Implementation: The Design in Use of Information Systems
Morten Hertzum

Data-Driven Personas
Bernard J. Jansen, Joni Salminen, Soon-gyo Jung, and Kathleen Guan

Worth-Focused Design, Book 2: Approaches, Context, and Case Studies
Gilbert Cockton

Worth-Focused Design, Book 1: Balance, Integration, and Generosity
Gilbert Cockton

Statistics for HCI: Making Sense of Quantitative Data
Alan Dix

Participatory Design
Susanne Bødker, Christian Dindler, Ole S. Iversen, and Rachel C. Smith

ISBN: 978-3-031-01107-8    Paperback
ISBN: 978-3-031-02235-7    PDF
ISBN: 978-3-031-00215-1    Hardcover

DOI 10.1007/978-3-031-02235-7

A Publication in the Springer series
*SYNTHESIS LECTURES ON HUMAN-CENTERED INFORMATICS*
Lecture #52
Series Editor: John M. Carroll, Penn State University

Series ISSN 1946-7680 Print 1946-7699 Electronic

# Participatory Design

Susanne Bødker, Christian Dindler, Ole S. Iversen, and Rachel C. Smith
Aarhus University, Denmark

*SYNTHESIS LECTURES ON HUMAN CENTERED INFORMATICS #52*

## ABSTRACT

This book introduces Participatory Design to researchers and students in Human–Computer Interaction (HCI). Grounded in four strong commitments, the book discusses why and how Participatory Design is important today. The book aims to provide readers with a practical resource, introducing them to the central practices of Participatory Design research as well as to key references. This is done from the perspective of Scandinavian Participatory Design. The book is meant for students, researchers, and practitioners who are interested in Participatory Design for research studies, assignments in HCI classes, or as part of an industry project. It is structured around 11 questions arranged in 3 main parts that provide the knowledge needed to get started with practicing Participatory Design. Each chapter responds to a question about defining, conducting, or the results of carrying out Participatory Design. The authors share their extensive experience of Participatory Design processes and thinking by combining historical accounts, cases, how-to process descriptions, and reading lists to guide further readings so as to grasp the many nuances of Participatory Design as it is practiced across sectors, countries, and industries.

## KEYWORDS

Interaction Design methods, Participatory Design process, perspectives, stakeholders, epistemology, toolbox

# Contents

# Preface:
# Eleven Important Questions for Participatory Design

Participatory Design, or PD as it is sometimes called, is a mysterious, inaccessible, and almost occult research approach practiced by a small group of high church priests in a Scandinavian and socialist research environment dating back the 1980s as a response to first–world problems belonging to the 1970s and 1980s. Participatory Design is a fairytale land in which end-user perspectives are valued without any considerations of everyday societal, economical, or social constraints. Participatory Design is only practiced in isolated, university-based projects that have been running for decades without any tangible outcomes but for research papers on a happy-go-lucky design process with lots of post-its, cardboard, and unproductive accounts of happy users. Participatory design is the icing on the cake that is oftentimes too expensive to conduct within the constraints of professional context.

If this is your impression of Participatory Design, we are here to prove you wrong.

If you are here without any presumptions on Participatory Design, we are here to provide you with a fairly easy way into the inspiring world of Participatory Design and its methods, tools, and techniques. In any case, you are very welcome.

The purpose of this book is to introduce Participatory Design and its core elements to Human–Computer Intersction (HCI) students. The book will take you through the process of conducting Participatory Design as part of your research study, your assignment in HCI classes, or as part of an industry project in a straightforward and accessible way. We will provide you with knowledge needed to get started in practicing Participatory Design. We point you in the direction of further readings if you want to fully grasp the many nuances and richness of Participatory Design as it is practiced in different countries or in industry, creative commons, or the health sector.

The purpose of this book emerged during a course at CHI 2016 in San José, CA (Bødker et al., 2016). Here, we organized a course on Participatory Design for HCI professionals. The course was a thorough introduction to Participatory Design for researchers and professionals within HCI. Our goal was to provide a condensed version of 40 years of Participatory Design in Scandinavia in a suitable format for HCI researchers and user-experience designers so that they would be capable of utilizing PD tools, methods, and techniques in their own practices. To our great surprise, the course was well attended, and our notebooks were full of questions posed by the audience during the four-hour course. Armed with post-it notes, pens, crayons, posters, and LEGO (yes, we are from

Denmark), the participants were situated in a Participatory Design landscape and solved a complex problem using tools and techniques common within Participatory Design. The participants
worked with a great commitment on the design challenge put in front of them. Meanwhile, the
course instructors (us) went from group to group posing unsolicited questions to the participants
and encouraging them to reflect on Participatory Design from their very different contexts of being
a trained HCI researcher, student, design practitioner, or something else. From this dialogue, we
learned a lot about the perception and assumptions of Participatory Design. Some of these are accounted for above. Reflecting on the course session, the instructors compared notes and gradually
developed an understanding of the course outcomes—especially with respect to what we gained
from the course activity. A few hours later, we had compiled a FAQ list which we all agreed on
would provide a great introduction to Participatory Design. The questions were:

1.  Can you define Participatory Design for me?

2.  What is Participatory Design?

3.  What can we learn from the history of Participatory Design?

4.  When and where is Participatory Design done?

5.  What are the activities and methods of Participatory Design?

6.  What are the tools and materials of Participatory Design?

7.  How is Participatory Design organized?

8.  How does one get started on Participatory Design and stay on track?

9.  What are the results of Participatory Design?

10. How does one sustain Participatory Design initiatives?

11. Why is Participatory Design important today?

In light of this list, the outline of this book is straightforward. Each chapter in the book will
revolve around one question from the FAQ, combining historical accounts, inspiring cases, how-to
process descriptions, and reading lists to propose directions for further study. We use cases that look
specifically at particular projects and address specific historic or contemporary matters of concern.
The cases are introduced where they are first used, but we return to many of them several times in
the book. Our aim is to provide you with Participatory Design insights that, hopefully, will take you
further into this particular and for us, highly productive, approach to the design of digital artifacts.

If you are already familiar with the questions on this FAQ, we advise you to read Simonsen
and Robertson's (2012) thorough account of Participatory Design. Schuler and Namioka (1993)

provide you with the historical accounts of Participatory Design and its roots from the United States and Scandinavia. ACM's library will provide you access to proceedings from Participatory Design conferences from 2004–2020 and if you are more interested in new trajectories within Participatory Design, Bannon et al. (2018a) make an excellent starting point in the special issue from TOCHI 2018. As a service to the Participatory Design community, Jesper Simonsen at Roskilde University has gathered all Participatory Design-related material since the very first PD conference in 1990 on the website http://pdcproceedings.org. This is an excellent website for pursuing different targets within the richness of Participatory Design literature.

## P.1    THE BOOK AND ITS OUTLINE

The book will address the above FAQ of 11 questions, using cases that are presented and developed as our arguments unfold. The book falls in three parts.

- PART I: Participatory Design: definition and history (Chapters 1–4)
  Here, we define Participatory Design and present its history and application areas.

- PART II: The Participatory Design toolbox (Chapters 5–8)
  The second part of the book presents frequently used methods, tools, and principles of organization in Participatory Design.

- PART III: Participatory Design results (Chapters 9–10)
  The third part discusses the expected results of a Participatory Design process and how the sustainability of these results is an integral part of the Participatory Design process itself.

Finally, we emphasize the importance of Participatory Design in relation to current societal challenges and emerging research topics in our concluding remarks presented in Chapter 11.

If you are a teacher of Human-Computer Interaction or Interaction Design at an interim level at a college or university, we hope you will find the book fitting into, or supplementing, your course as the focus of 3–4 weeks of class, structured around the mentioned three parts. The book is focused on giving students of HCI the practical means to use in their future work whether in industry or research. Hence, it does not cover all the newest research findings in every nook and corner of Participatory Design.

We have chosen to introduce eight cases of very different kinds to exemplify the discussions and methods in the chapters. The case descriptions can, however, be read independent of the text where they are first used, and we have hence chosen to format them as "side boxes" that are spread across the book. This means that the reader can find them and read them independently. The chapters also have "read more" boxes for the interested reader who wants to know more. In these we identify central, more general readings as well as elaboration of specific examples.

The material presented in this book has roots in Simonsen and Robertson (2012) as well as many of our own writings over the years, not least of all Bødker, et al. (2017), Bødker and Kyng (2018), Bannon et al. (2018a and b), Bohøj et al. (2011), Smith and Iversen (2018), Frauenberger et al. (2015), Brodersen Hansen et al. (2019), Dindler and Iversen (2014), Iversen and Dindler (2014), Bossen et al. (2016a), and Bødker and Zander (2015). In many instances, further and more research-oriented arguments can be found in these works, and we recommend looking there for details.

## P.2 WHO ARE WE?

The authors of this Synthesis Lecture all work at Aarhus University in Denmark. From this vantage point, we have been involved with Participatory Design research and teaching over many years. Our own educational backgrounds cover topics from computer science to anthropology. At Aarhus University, Participatory Design is taught in undergraduate and graduate programs in computer science, information studies, and digital design and we have used our experiences from teaching such classes in preparing this book. Being of different ages, some of us have been involved in early Participatory Design projects such as the UTOPIA project, and others have been very active in the Participatory Design Conference (PDC) community recently.

It is important for us to acknowledge that this book would never have happened without the (often long-term) collaboration, and endless debates and discussions, with our many coauthors. They include Liam Bannon, Jeffrey Bardzell, Morten Kyng, Joan Greenbaum, Kim Halskov, Claus Bossen, Morten Bohøj, Nikolaj Borchorst, Matthias Korn, Pär-Ola Zander, Joanna Saad-Sulonen, Nicolai Brodersen Hansen, Ditte Basballe, Chris Frauenberger, Judith Good, Geraldine Fitzpatrick, Ben Schouten, Peter Dalsgaard, Clemens Klokmose, Henrik Korsgaard, Daria Loi, Eva Eriksson, Heike Winschiers-Theophilus, Asnath Paula Kambunga, Maarten Van Mechelen, and Pelle Ehn. Peter Lyle and Maurizio Teli helped us summarize their Commonfare project as Case 3. We sincerely thank Shaowen Bardzell, Chris Frauenberger and John Vines for comments on earlier versions of this book, and Marianne Dammand Iversen for helping with our language. This writing process was made possible through the interdisciplinary research center PIT and the Center for Computational Thinking and Design at Aarhus University, Denmark.

Now, we will return to the FAQ list. We will start with the first question of our FAQ list to firmly position our particular take on Participatory Design as it is unfolded in this book. We devote our effort to introducing curious students and scholars to the methods, practices, and perspectives of Scandinavian Participatory Design. We hope that the book will make a good starting point for university students, researchers, and professionals interested in practicing Participatory Design methods and techniques, and wanting to expand their existing design capability and vocabulary with Participatory Design.

# PART I

# Participatory Design: Definition and History

CHAPTER 1

# Can You Define Participatory Design for Me?

We start our discussion of the 11 questions with exploring a definition of Participatory Design. Asking for one definition of Participatory Design is, however, easier said than done as we shall see. We will start with how various textbooks define Participatory Design and focus our definition from there.

## 1.1    TEXTBOOK DEFINITIONS OF PARTICIPATORY DESIGN

*The Handbook of Participatory Design* (Simonsen and Robertson, 2012) defines Participatory Design as:

> *"a process of investigating, understanding, reflecting upon, establishing, developing, and supporting mutual learning between multiple participants in collective 'reflection-in-action'* (Schön, 1983). *The participants typically undertake the two principal roles of users and designers where the designers strive to learn the realities of the users' situation while the users strive to articulate their desired aims and learn appropriate technological means to obtain them"* (p.2).

Here, Participatory Design is primarily a concern for:

- designers working together with people;

- reflecting together to accomplish a shared goal;

- a process characterized by mutual learning; and

- both the design outcome and the learning process are legitimate end-goals for a Participatory Design process.

Participatory Design was never infused into HCI textbooks with the same clarity as in Simonsen and Robertson (2012). In early versions, Preece, Rogers, and Sharp try to motivate why Participatory Design is relevant, beyond the need to work directly with users, but in later versions they simply seem to have given up their attempt at such explanations (Preece et al., 2019). Shneiderman and Plaisant (4th international edition, 2005) start with 1.5 pages of what seems to be an apology for even bringing up the topic: *"Many authors have urged participatory design strategies, but the concept is controversial. The arguments in favor suggest that more user involvement brings more accurate information about tasks and an opportunity for users to influence design decisions."* On the other hand, the book points out that extensive user involvement may be costly and generate antagonism from people who are not involved. The book, and its later editions, argue for careful selection of users. Benyon (2013), when talking about Participative Design, takes his main starting point from Mumford's (1997) British sociotechnical tradition and points out that there are roots in Scandinavia as well, in making an argument for why interconnected social and technical development is important. However, Benyon also refrains from defining the essential elements of Participatory Design in HCI.

In all of the books analyzed for this synthesis lecture, there are attempts at explaining how to do design by applying methods for direct collaboration with users. While it is important for HCI at large to have methods to actively engage directly with future users of technology, such methods are by now also quite mainstream and shared with what is known as both co-design and user-centered design. In Participatory Design, however, it is important to understand that there are also other ways of working with users, some of whom are not the future direct users of the technologies while others may be.

Participatory Design comes in many flavors. The biannual Participatory Design Conferences provide a large variety of Participatory Design, in action, integrating pragmatic, business-oriented, political, and activist cases and research. It is beyond the scope of this book to tidy up the messiness of methods and toolboxes, or to provide a comprehensive account for the many coexisting approaches that embody Participatory Design. In that respect, it is not our aim to be comprehensive in every area of Participatory Design. On the contrary, we have written the book from the particular perspective of the Scandinavian Participatory Design approach that we have been actively engaged in cultivating.

With this synthesis lecture we deliberately want to move the understanding of Participatory Design beyond methods for direct user engagement and mend the situation by offering explanations and motivations needed for working with Participatory Design in HCI teaching and research. We acknowledge the definition of Participatory Design as provided by Simonson and Robertson (2012), but see the need for a more elaborate introduction to this design approach especially suitable for HCI students and practitioners.

## 1.2    TOWARD OUR DEFINITION OF PARTICIPATORY DESIGN

Our particular Participatory Design approach dates back to the Scandinavian heritage as one among many other vibrant and interesting Participatory Design practices worldwide. However, we find the above definitions too limited as we shall see below.

Participatory Design is a concern for engaging human beings in the design of future technology. Participation is emphasized as a way by which people can influence digital technologies that will change their work practices or everyday life. Similar to Participatory Design, other approaches such as user-centered design, co-design, user-experience design, or experience-based design also entail elements of participation. But, as we will argue in this book, there is more to Participatory Design than participation (Bødker and Iversen, 2002). In fact, participation is only vaguely declaring the qualities of genuine Participatory Design work. Demystifying Participatory Design is one of the main concerns in this book, as is providing future designers with a concrete starting point for embracing the emphatical qualities of genuine Participatory Design work. By talking about genuine Participatory Design work we emphasize that people are engaged in designing their future technologies not as "users" but as human beings with the full faculty of skillfulness, emotions, concerns, beliefs, and grounding values that make us human.

In Participatory Design, people actively engage in the process of imagining their own future work practices, communities, or everyday life through the design of digital technology. This is a process of mutual learning between people and professional designers that are capable of translating the imagined futures into digital technology. In this respect, Participatory Design is a process of negotiating possible futures and personal or societal values, and from that starting point shaping new digital technologies to support human lives.

In these processes, we commit to working with people, groups or organizations to explore how future technologies might support their imagined futures. As voiced by Bødker (2003). we do this not so much to build people's future technology but to help them realize that they have a choice (p. 89). Because having a choice means that people reflect on their own relationship to digital technology, on the intentionality and anticipated use that are inherently embedded in digital technology, while being mindful of the fact that when it comes to digital technology, we have a choice. In this respect, Participatory Design is directed toward a tangible design outcome, most often in relation to a future application, system or hardware, and embraces at the same time a critical and inquisitive approach to digital technology among its participants.

Participatory design in our **definition** includes activities where users, designers, and researchers collaborate toward shared goals. *Mutual learning* between these groups is hence important as is the emphasis that Participatory Design starts with the *current practices* of people in groups and organizations and uses *future alternatives* for joint reflection and action, in critical and inclusive ways. It is important to understand that mutual learning is not just a simple relation between individuals. We focus on *empowerment of people* not only as individuals but as part of their groups and communities, both as they are currently established and for the (possible) future. Whether in the workplace or elsewhere, such settings are full of conflicts that design as such cannot solve, even though they need to be handled in the processes. Seeing human beings as *skillful* and *resourceful* in the development of their future joint practices sets focus on Participatory Design as a set of *emancipatory practices*, also in situations where power is not equally balanced. In this way, Participatory Design is committed to *democracy* (see also, Section 2.1).

This chapter discussed definitions of Participatory Design and ends with a tentative definition that we return to. In Chapter 2, we offer a brief tour of Participatory Design to set the scene for its methods and processes.

# CHAPTER 2

# What Is Participatory Design?

Participatory Design, User-Centered Design, People Centered Design, User-oriented Design, Human-Centered Design, Contextual Design, Co-design, Cooperative Design, Experience Design, or just simply Interaction Design. The literature on design approaches that incorporate elements of people engagement in design of computer technologies is promoted under different headings and in different research communities. Being new to design approaches, the differences between these different trajectories might seem confusing and perhaps even insignificant in relation to a design task at hand. However, there is a very good reason for seeking alignment between the approach you choose and the design task at hand. In the following, we will continue to extract the defining elements of Participatory Design. We do this to provide an overview of Participatory Design, to emphasize its uniqueness, and to point ahead to other chapters for further explanations of concepts, history, methods, and domains of application.

To answer the question of what is Participatory Design, this chapter provides a brief introduction to the main concepts, approaches, and ideas that will be developed further throughout the the book. In particular, we will sketch answers to the following questions.

- What are the commitments of Participatory Design?

- What characterizes participation in Participatory Design?

- What is Participatory Design compared to other design approaches?

- What are the essentials in the Participatory Design legacy?

- Where is Participatory Design applied?

- What are the core elements of a Participatory Design toolbox?

## 2.1 WHAT ARE THE COMMITMENTS OF PARTICIPATORY DESIGN?

Participatory Design is concerned with the needs, wants, and desires of users, both as individuals and as a whole. However, it is not concerned as such with building technologies that users like or are pleasing. On the contrary, sometimes part of what Participatory Design does is to help users understand possibilities and alternatives, and what it takes to get there.

First of all, Participatory Design takes its starting point from the values and concerns of particular groups. Their needs and desires may often be in contrast to those of other groups and hence such tensions need to be considered. Second, engaging with a particular group, in a process of mutual learning and in order to empower it, also means showing alternatives from which the practice of the users may move in different directions. So, there may not be one best solution anyway, and the choices made have consequences for the community of users, as well as for others around them.

Fundamentally, Participatory Design views human beings as active human actors, in contrast to human factors (Bannon, 1991), and classical organizational models where humans are cogwheels in the machine (see, e.g., Morgan, 1986). Hence, empowering is fundamentally about building up resources for people to act skillfully when it comes to development, introduction, and use of computer technology.

Participatory Design embraces ways of working with people who are in some form or another going to be the end-users of the technology. But it does not stop there. Participatory Design works with various ways in which people can represent their peers, *qua* skills, particular insights, elected representation, etc. Hence, building up resources also involves the build-up of communication and education for these peers, both locally and often also to a wider community. Participating in design processes is participating in political processes characterized by different values, and different resources and means for exercising power.

It is the basis of a democratic concern to empower people through design and development processes where alternatives are developed to illustrate and counterbalance mainstream solutions or technologies proposed by management or other more resourceful counterparts. The learning processes as such give more people access to understanding the possibilities and problems of technology. The way Participatory Design understands empowering and learning stands on two legs. One is a matter of helping people act differently or better with technology, and understanding the technology better by using it and acting with it.

Participatory Design emphasizes prototyping and hands-on experience again and again. Therefore, the second leg is communication and the development of how we talk about technology, when we design it, and when we use it.

Hence, empowerment points to a basic concern for democracy. However, it also sets a political scene for the design processes, and this means that design needs to concern itself with politics at many levels, from national and international concerns regarding what technology should and shouldn't do, politics of various kinds in the use domains, or politics of the design process as such. These latter include decision processes across management and labor, challenges of assigning resources to various parts of the design process, etc.

In this framing, there are several arguments why Participatory Design emphasizes the process over a specific product. The process is important for empowering and mutual learning, is important because of politics, and is important specifically because it makes better sense to understand the products/designs developed as tentative parts of the process rather than as THE solution to things (see also Floyd, 1987). This process view lets participants explore the tentative products, e.g., in the form of prototypes, against wants and desires, as well as against resource and political constraints and possibilities. It allows for building and exploring alternatives.

In the current technological landscape it is almost always the case that people are users of some technologies that are then replaced, extended, or substituted with others. This means that new technological solutions are built and implemented into an existing landscape that it then changes, as a result of the design process, and with the unpredictability that such processes entail. No design process, even Participatory Design, can fully predict the changes ahead, hence introducing new technologies is often the starting point for yet new change and design processes. This way of understanding the relationship between design and use is sometimes called infrastructuring, and Pipek and Wulf (2009) talk about the points where technologies move from being "in design" to being "in use" as "points of infrastructuring." Ultimately, to empower users to participate in both design and use, infrastructuring is important. And Participatory Design is concerned with exactly that.

Based upon this background we have identified four strong commitments that add to our definition of Participatory Design in Section 1.2.

1. Participatory Design is committed to *democracy*, at the workplace and beyond.

2. It is concerned with the *empowerment* of people through the *processes of design*.

3. Participatory Design aims for *emancipatory practices* rooted in *mutual learning* between designers and people.

4. Fundamentally, this is done by seeing human beings as *skillful* and *resourceful* in the development of their future practices.

## 2.2    WHAT CHARACTERIZES PARTICIPATION IN PARTICIPATORY DESIGN?

Participatory Design is, in our view, not about working with and making a small group of future direct users happy, but what is it then? In some instances, Participatory Design is used when engaging with future users locally and in a particular context, and many of the methods mentioned work for that type of situation. However, most often design is not only a local endeavor but, as PD shows, bridges between the direct, hands-on participation of people and larger project issues.

The connection between the local participation and larger project issues is discussed by Grønbæk et al., (2017) regarding the difference between how Participatory Design may be deployed in product development, in-organization development, and consultancy-type design processes. Bødker et al. (2017) discussed Participatory Design in very political, public organizations where activities and decisions are needed at many levels and with many different participants to make the actual participation of future users happen. They emphasized that with Participatory Design, participation is also when workers and citizens are engaged in these larger project issues as representatives of their peers.

Bødker and Grønbæk (1991a) discussed how participants may be selected to represent their peers, either based on volunteering, skill, specific organizational roles, or for reasons of trust among peers (e.g., representation through the role as union representative). They advise against thinking of management as being able to represent workers, because management lacks the detailed, everyday understanding of the activities to be designed for. No matter which type of representation is used, resources must be considered and set aside for the participants. Such resources include their time, their possibilities of making independent preparations, etc. Also, ways for participants to keep the connections to their peers must be considered, in terms of time, including the possibilities of having meetings with peers, for paid work time, and for other peers to take over work. The sharing of information is important, and representatives must be able to share project matters with their peers (and, e.g., not be requested to sign non-disclosure agreements). These matters are central for Participatory Design and must be discussed and negotiated as part of the planning of a Participatory Design project, as will be discussed further in Chapter 5.

## 2.3    HOW DOES PARTICIPATORY DESIGN COMPARE TO OTHER APPROACHES?

We introduced this chapter with a long list of distinct design approaches which all include a certain element of people participation during the design process. Comparing Participatory Design to other design approaches can be difficult because the term "Participatory Design" is used in a variety of ways in research and practice. For some people, Participatory Design simply refers to design that, in one way or another, involves non-designer people taking part in design activities. In this understanding, Participatory Design is arguably very similar to co-design and many practices within Interaction Design. For others, Participatory Design refers to a tradition where democracy and empowerment are central tenets and design thus becomes a political engagement. To complicate matters further, this uneven use of terms not only applies to Participatory Design but also to practices such as "co-design," "user centered design," or "interaction design."

Sanders and Stappers (2008) provide a landscape of different design approaches differentiating between them by use of two parameters:

- the extent to which the process is led by design or by research and

- the extent to which participants are seen as "subjects" or "partners" in the design process.

Here, Participatory Design is depicted as the only human-centered design approach that is solely seeing participants as design partners both in projects led by research and design. The landscape provided by Sanders and Stappers derives back from 2008. Although heavily cited in Interaction Design literature, the landscape of human-centered design approaches changes rapidly and repeatedly as new approaches emerge and former approaches merge in new research contributions within HCI, Interaction Design, and related areas. These dynamics are also found in contemporary Participatory Design.

Through the years, there has been an important exchange between Participatory Design and other approaches to design. Participatory practices have become commonplace in some parts of HCI, and design approaches used in research and industry often feature participatory elements. Similarly, Participatory Design has evolved to embrace ideas from other approaches including tools and techniques for sketching and prototyping (see Chapter 7). As such, clear-cut boundaries between Participatory Design and related disciplines are difficult to draw. However, taking a step back and mindfully reviewing the legacy of the Participatory Design movement discloses the uniqueness of the design approach that has been reinterpreted and revitalized at the biannual Participatory Design conference since the early 1990s.

## 2.4     WHAT ARE THE ESSENTIALS IN THE PARTICIPATORY DESIGN LEGACY?

In order to explain further the four strong commitments and their reasons behind them, we now focus on the historical legacy and how the commitments came about. The history of Participatory Design is explained further in Chapter 3 but for now we will stay with the strong commitments and how they came about from the start.

Historically, Participatory Design was developed in order to help white- and blue-collar workers in traditional industries understand and learn about possible alternatives to the technologies imposed on them by management. The point was to democratically balance and counter the development processes of management (Ehn and Sandberg, 1979), and hence there is a fundamental commitment to workplace democracy in Participatory Design.

In this process, however, the researchers also learned that this could not be done in classical expert processes where alternative solutions were brought in from the outside (Nygaard and Bergo, 1975). Working actively with the workers was a necessity for empowering them to understand and make choices, and hence an important focus for Participatory Design became that of empowering people through the process of design.

These thoughts were in later projects developed further into a strategy of mutual learning (Ehn and Kyng, 1987), where it was emphasized that it is necessary for users to actively partner with designers and researchers. It is equally necessary for designers and researchers to partner with the users to learn the daily practices of the community for which they are to design [this is parallel to the learning relationship and partnership model proposed by Beyer and Holtzblatt in Contextual Design (Holtzblatt and Beyer, 1997)]. Historically, an important source of inspiration for such thoughts was Freire's book *Pedagogy of the Oppressed* (Freire, 1970). This book has had new attention in the HCI literature recently (e.g., Ghoshal and Bruckman, 2019). Central to Participatory Design is therefore an emancipatory practice deriving from the mutual learning of designers and people.

The idea that we need to understand technology by acting with it has roots in Activity Theory, as well as Heidegger, Dewey, and others who in various forms talked about tacit and procedural knowledge (see Ehn, 1988), and the concern for developing a shared language was deeply embedded in Nygaard's early thoughts scrutinized, e.g., by Ehn (1988) using Wittgenstein's language games understanding. A shared language regarding technology use and development in the particular context is hence an important part of the resource build-up. Hence, Participatory Design sees human beings as skillful and these skills provide crucial aspects to a design process.

Chapter 3 provides a deeper understanding of the Participatory Design legacy and the concern for skillfulness, mutual learning, emancipation, and democracy. Here, we will point to some of the current domains and application areas in which Participatory Design has been used successfully throughout the past decades.

## 2.5    WHERE IS PARTICIPATORY DESIGN APPLIED?

Participatory Design has been used in settings of a small group of future users, in a setting where no computers are used at all. However, it is our starting point here that we deal with the design of computer technology and its use at many levels, from society via organizations and non-governmental organizations (NGOs) to use by smaller groups and even by the individual user, in settings where some technology is already there. Individual users are connected with these other levels through the purposes of what they do when they use the technology, the outcome of these activities, and the practices, routines, and other means that they share among them. We will give examples of how this can be done in the cases presented in the coming chapters.

Whereas Participatory Design was originally developed for workplace contexts and to provide alternatives in terms of process and products in such contexts, in more recent years it has been successfully utilized in a wide range of domains and contexts which bear witness to the fact that the concern for democracy, skillfulness, and emancipation has wider implications than the workplace. You can find inspiration to current research on Participatory Design in relation to participatory engagement with cultural heritage, engagement with indigenous populations, learning in formal and informal contexts, civic and public settings, government and citizens relations, communities, children's learning and empowerment, families, elderly people, vulnerable communities, healthcare, refugees, and more (see Chapter 4).

There are many ways of talking about the computer technology that gets designed. Traditionally, this has often been addressed as systems to address the interconnectedness of various parts, software to address programs, and architectures, in contrast to hardware and devices. Apps and interfaces are more recent words for parts of this, and we prefer to talk about computer artifacts to emphasize that these are, on the one hand, built by human beings and, on the other hand, brought into use and often appropriated by users to fit local needs, routines, and outcomes they make. Computer artifacts are designed, infrastructured, appropriated by users and exist in ecologies with other computer artifacts used by overlapping groups and communities of users.

We will unfold some of these application areas of Participatory Design in more detail in Chapter 4. Here, we will provide an overview of the repertoire of methods and techniques most frequently used in Participatory Design to scaffold a mutual learning process between designers and participants.

## 2.6 WHAT ARE THE CORE ELEMENTS OF A PARTICIPATORY DESIGN TOOLBOX?

A good starting point for conducting Participatory Design is to familiarize with the different activities, tools, and techniques of Participatory Design. It is important to understand that various tools and techniques are not exclusively used in Participatory Design. They can also be found in other approaches such as co-design, experience-centered design, or conventional Interaction Design. What makes activities, tools, and techniques distinct in Participatory Design is how they are utilized in alignment with the core elements: to support mutual learning, democracy, empowerment of end-users, and to acknowledge the skillfulness of all people involved in the design process. We have devoted three chapters (Chapters 6–8) to further develop the presentation of the Participatory Design activities, tools, and techniques.

### 2.6.1 WORKSHOPS

Often Participatory Design is happening within a design process that is connected together through various activities, in particular workshops where users and designers collaborate. Workshops are described in Chapter 6 as a main activity of Participatory Design. The overall process is set up to take steps and build up and sustain a shared understanding and technological basis across people and activities. Workshops have been important to Participatory Design from the start, inspired by political activism (Nygaard and Bergo, 1975) and, e.g., the future workshops developed by Jungk and Müllert (1987) for participation in urban development. Today, we have available a wide variety of workshop forms to be used at various stages of the design process, as we discuss later in Chapters 6 and 7.

### 2.6.2    COOPERATIVE PROTOTYPING AND PROTOTYPES

Participatory Design emphasizes that hands-on experience with the future is important, and hence Participatory Design utilizes various forms of prototyping, under the main activity of cooperative prototyping [Chapter 6; see also Ehn and Kyng (1991) and Bødker and Grønbæk, (1991a)]. Prototypes are used experimentally and exploratively in different stages, from such supporting visions and idea generation among designers and users, to help users explore and assess specific details of future work processes. Prototyping may support the work with alternatives at large, including also the exploration of different alternative futures, as well as, e.g., different alternative forms of interaction with a particular design (see Chapter 6).

### 2.6.3    ITERATIVE DEVELOPMENT

Iterative development is important because software engineering in general points out that it is impossible to map out all technical requirements in one shot, and build for them (see, e.g., Floyd, 1987). This is equally true for use-oriented requirements where it is difficult to anticipate future use, and where hands-on exploration is necessary as a step to further grasp the future and the next steps to explore. To some extent, prototypes may hence build on top of each other but they may also be used to explore different parts or alternatives, be this for different use situations or forms of interaction of underlying technical constructs.

### 2.6.4    MOCK-UPS

What we call prototypes may come in many forms, depending on what they are needed for, but in almost all instances they are not intended to be complete, running technological systems (see Chapter 6, cooperative prototyping). Mock-ups (Ehn and Kyng, 1991) and paper prototypes allow for quick iteration and understandable material for all involved in the Participatory Design processes. Running computational prototypes with limited functionality and/or Wizard of Oz support makes the exploration of more complex use processes and interaction more realistic (Bødker and Grønbæk, 1991a). In some instances, prototypes can also be programs that may work almost like the solution intended (perhaps with limited data, or, e.g., without security or data validation). Such may in some cases be necessary in order to explore, e.g., wider work-organizational or collaboration issues in use, and to illustrate alternative processes and products (see Chapter 7).

In this manner, working with alternatives is not only an overall target of Participatory Design, it also penetrates the toolbox at many levels. At the same time, it is important to remember that this level of methods for direct collaboration between participants is not all that is happening in Participatory Design. These activities need to be connected with political, democratic, and organizational processes that reach out from the local community in various ways that we discuss.

## 2.7    SUMMARY

This chapter presented a condensed version of what Participatory Design is. In the coming chapters we will provide more details, regarding both its means and methods and its participants. We have pointed to the four strong commitments, in particular the importance of empowering the users as a cornerstone for Participatory Design, in comparison with various user-centered methods where the primary purpose is for the experts to learn from users. We have presented mutual learning as the underlying principle through which exploratory processes involving users and designers may address new technologies and their uses.

We have outlined participation as more than simple and direct collaboration between users and designers. We have also defined Participatory Design as a distinct design approach but also outlined the similarities and differences between Participatory Design and other approaches that are in various ways still concerned with future users of technology. We have delineated Participatory Design in terms of its unique legacy and some of the domains where it is applied, and we have pointed to the core elements of a Participatory Design toolbox where iteration, and hands-on experience are important, even though they need supplementing with other elements as we return to in Chapters 4, 9, and 10. Many of the points addressed in this initial chapter will be centerpieces in the chapters that follow.

**Read More**

To learn more about Participatory Design, and in particular its methods, *The Handbook of Participatory Design* (Simonsen and Robertson, 2012) is a good place to start, as is the older *Design at Work* book (Greenbaum and Kyng, 1991). Contemporary cases, concepts, and discussions can be found in proceedings of PDC (Participatory Design Conference) in particular, but also conferences like CHI (the ACM SigCHI conference), DIS (Designing Interactive Systems), and Communities and Technologies have relevant papers and cases.

CHAPTER 3

# What Can We Learn from the History of Participatory Design?

At first sight Participatory Design is characterized by the active participation of users in the design process. However, as we have discussed, the commitment to Participatory Design reaches far beyond active user engagement. In Chapter 2, we learned that Participatory Design has four strong commitments: (workplace) democracy; empowerment of people through the process of design; emancipatory practice rooted in mutual learning of designers and people; and seeing human beings as skillful and resourceful in the development of their future practices.

In this chapter we offer a more detailed account of how Participatory Design emerged and grew its strong commitments. To do this, we will provide a historical overview of Participatory Design into four eras:

- Era 1. (1970–1985) From experts to activist researchers

- Era 2. (1985–1992) Getting more out of the users

- Era 3. (1992–2013) Multiplicity of method and foci

- Era 4. (2014– ) Reaching out and regaining political teeth

In characterizing the four eras of Participatory Design research it is important to keep in mind that one does not replace the other and, hence, research lives on and each era talks more to what dominated the field at a particular time. However, the four eras provide a valuable account of how Participatory Design has been motivated, adapted, restructured, and reshaped when confronted with emerging societal and technological challenges. Moreover, history provides an important source for better understanding how Participatory Design differs significantly from other related human-centered design approaches and why user participation is only half way to Participatory Design.

Figure 3.1 provides an overview of the four eras of Participatory Design accounting for the main changes in relation to the researcher (or designer), the participants engaged in the design process, the objectives of the design process and the tools needed. We dedicate the rest of the chapter to unfold the history of Participatory Design in greater detail to fully unpack the distinctness of this design approach.

| Eras | Researcher | Participants | Objective | Tools |
|---|---|---|---|---|
| Era 1 (1970–1985) | Breaking away from the role of expert acting as an activist researcher | Educating blue and white collar workers (and their unions) to engage in the decision-making around digital technology | Workplace democracy: Balancing power and agency among managers and workers at a time when increasingly technology | Working groups and workshops |
| Era 2 (1985–1992) | Research on understanding "human actors" in human–computer interaction | From users to people. Focus on skillful human beings acting in specific contexts and activities together | Understanding human actors when introducing new digital technology at the workplaces | Co-design and contextual design |
| Era 3 (1993–2013) | Researchers from many other disciplines take up methods from Participatory Design | Empowerment of users beyond the workplace and with respect to individual needs | "Doing good" for people engaging with digital technology | Development of a multiplicity of methods and techniques for understanding users and use |
| Era 4 (2014–now) | Reconnecting to the political responsibilities in design | Engaging various people. Local and global development projects as critical alternatives | Rekindling the political aspects of Participatory Design | Scaling and sustaining Participatory Design projects |

Figure 3.1: The four eras of Participatory Design and their characteristics.

## 3.1    ERA 1: FROM EXPERT TO ACTIVIST RESEARCHERS (1970–1985)

Participatory Design started in the 1970s motivated by the introduction of information technology in the workplace. It sought to balance power and agency among managers and workers at a time when computer technology was being introduced in the workplace at great pace. This was, however, at the same time as in all of Northern Europe a majority of workers belonged to trade unions, collective bargaining was on the rise, and social welfare was politically in focus.

In this space both labor unions and groups of academics were at loss with how to impact the introduction of computer technology in the workplace. Methods and insights were simply not there. Hence, the motivation for this early work was an attempt to activate scientific knowledge better to counter and balance the insights of management. Researchers took an interest in challenges different from mainstream possibilities and problems, and unions were seen as one of many possible kinds of sources and collaborators in this respect. This development was predominant in many parts of the Western world, and, in particular, the Scandinavian countries and in Germany. In these countries, workers, their organizations, and researchers of many kinds were seeking to establish methods to influence the development of information technology both locally, nationally, and internationally, for the above reasons.

This early era of what came to be known as Participatory Design happened in several projects, starting with three Scandinavian "sister" projects, NJMF, Case 1, (Nygaard and Bergo, 1975), DUE (Kyng and Mathiassen, 1980, 1982), and Demos (Ehn and Sandberg, 1979, 1983). These projects emphasized local union activism and developed models for negotiation and collaboration between unions/union representatives and management. This was seen as a way to impact the development and introduction of technology in workplaces, hence creating an impact on society. These projects were breaking away from models where researchers were brought in as experts and instead activated models of working groups and workshops where union members were active participants. Clement and Van den Besselaar (1993) in their summary of early Participatory Design projects point to the importance of workers getting access to information; getting the opportunity to take independent positions on issues; and getting included in the processes of decision making in processes where appropriate participatory methods are available with sufficient organizational and technological flexibility.

These projects also increased the awareness that technical alternatives were lacking and needed. Creating technological alternatives became a focus of the Florence (Bjerknes and Bratteteig, 1987) and Utopia projects, Case 2, (Bødker et al., 1985, 1987; Ehn, 2014). Both of these projects moved their focus away from the local engagement in workplaces and worked with central unions (of nurses, and graphics workers). The Utopia project in particular was motivated by its concern for technological alternatives, but became known also for its design methods that focused on mock-ups, prototypes, and workshops for users' hands-on experience (Ehn and Kyng, 1991).

It is important to notice that projects and activities like the ones described continued, and e.g., the Swedish labor union TCO (Swedish Confederation for Professional Employees) had great international success with certifying display screens, to the extent where the TCO label for healthy working conditions became world known, without much attention to where the label came from (Boivie, 2007).

In summary, the early era was breaking away from seeing the researcher or designer as an expert to becoming an activist and collaborating researcher and designer who was concerned with computer-based alternatives whether through mutual learning locally in the workplace or more with more potent central actors, always with a view to power imbalance, resources, and negotiation. In this manner, our four strong commitments take their starting point in the results from these projects when it comes to *democracy*, at the workplace, *empowerment* of people through the processes of design, *emancipatory practices* rooted in mutual learning between designers and people, and the perspective of human beings as *skillful* and *resourceful* in the development of their future practices.

**Case 1: NJMF**

The first era of projects included the NJMF (1971–73), Demos (1975–79), and DUE (1977–80). They were situated in each Scandinavian country and did research on:

- the impact of computer use at workplaces;

- the formulation of demands regarding computer technology in organizations;

- the formulation of agreements between employers and unions, regulating the introduction and use of;

- technology at the workplaces, the need for knowledge, teaching material, and courses among workers and union members;

- new frameworks for worker influence, by addressing worker controlled resources; and

- new models of negotiations (Bødker and Kyng, 2018).

The projects developed with different emphasis, but an important part of all of them was cooperation with the local trade unions to focus on the pros and cons of deployment of computers at work.

The **NJMF** (Norwegian Iron and Metalworkers' Union) project was the first and served as inspiration for all of them. It started as an expert investigation where researchers worked to consider how unions could influence the above issues. However, it became clear that a traditional expert investigation would make very little impact in the actual factories and workplaces where influence on technology was at stake.

Nygaard and Bergo (1975) found inspiration from the work in the Norwegian anti-EU movement, which had succeeded through local workgroups in workplaces across Norway. Hence, the focus of NJMF was shifted to an active cooperation between researchers and workers. As was the case in this political counterpart, the approach was bottom-up, building on people's own experiences, and providing resources that enabled them to act in their current situations. These ways of working are in many ways the start of Participatory Design methods as we still know them today.

The NJMF project, however, did more than these local working groups. Largely, the project pointed to computers as managerial instruments of increased control, as well as to the need for training and education for workers on the shop floor (e.g., Nygaard and Bergo, 1975). It systematically analyzed and debated new technologies being brought into particular plants: A new production planning system was shown to inevitably lead to more overtime work. Shop-floor terminals to be used were shown to only allow data entry, and not offer workers status information at the shop floor.

With both NJMF, Demos, and DUE, the Participatory Design's focus was on local action and negotiations based on central union support consisting of the development of teaching materials and support for negotiations. Hence, the role of the central unions became to produce these materials and to support the processes.

**Case 2: Utopia**

The Utopia project is the most well-known early era project, known for its development of methods as well as its commitment to exploration of future technologies. Pelle Ehn sums up the basis of the first era project, Utopia (Ehn, 2014): *"focusing on democracy—and worker participation—actively searching—alternative futures—through collaborative—design things—at the time when computers entered the shop floor—threatening to deskill workers—and tighten managerial control."*

The Utopia project was a Scandinavian research project carried out by the Swedish Center for Working Life, The Royal Technical University in Sweden, and Aarhus University in Denmark in the first half of the 1980s. Utopia is a Scandinavian acronym for "Training, Technology and Product in a Perspective of Quality of Work." Utopia was a collaboration between the researchers and the Nordic Graphic Workers' Union in an attempt to create technologies that were not deskilling workers, but rather made the best of, and supported, their skills in newspaper production. Technological alternatives were important to the researchers who were witnessing that computer technology was mainly used for routinization of jobs while also leading to low-quality products, be these newspapers or documents in many kinds of work. And alternatives were important to the unions because they needed to be able to point to other possible ways of using technology when, e.g., negotiating with management in various situations. This was at a time where the union movement had a strong say in the development of the Nordic welfare state, and a further reason why the collaboration between researchers and unions was seen as beneficial by both parties.

The project came close to producing a computer technology that could be marketed (called TIPS) but for various economical and societal reasons this part of the project fell apart. In the end, the influx of cheaper standard technology from North America was simply unavoidable, leading basically to the disappearance of newspaper production as skilled work across the world.

Instead, Utopia is today well known for the Participatory Design methods it developed, in particular focusing on technological alternatives (both software and hardware, see Figures 6.1 and 6.2), tacit knowledge, hands-on experience, simulation games, low-tech prototypes, and mock-ups.

The Utopia project combined research and development with a small group of skilled typographic workers, with detailed field studies in particular newspaper plants, interdisciplinary research, and a strong dissemination effort consisting of:

- several conferences with a wide group of newspaper workers and their union representatives;

- a tight collaboration with the Nordic Graphic Workers' Union and the national printers' and typographers' unions in the Nordic countries; and

- a newsletter (*Graffiti*) produced with regular intervals, and with the summary report (*Graffiti 7*, Bødker et al., 1985) distributed to all union members in their respective national languages. *Graffiti 7* produced in 70,000 copies in 5 languages (Danish, Finnish, Norwegian, Swedish, and English).

## 3.2   ERA 2: GETTING MORE OUT OF THE USERS (1985–1998)

In the latter half of the 1980s, a number of activities led to Participatory Design getting its name and making the journey across to North America: The North America-based organization called Computer Professionals for Social Responsibility took an interest in Participatory Design and the first Participatory Design conference was established under the auspices of Lucy Suchman.

This move across the Atlantic was also motivated in the so-called second wave of HCI that introduced a focus on real activities, real use of computers by real people, as a replacement for the first wave's modeling of people and their activities. The first wave approach was model-driven and focused on the human beings as subjects to be studied, from the outside by the detached researcher through rigid guidelines, formal methods, and systematic testing, as discussed by Bannon (1991).

Bannon talked about the move to the second wave as *"from human factors to human actors."* At that time, Participatory Design was critical toward human factors thinking in general because of the view of the human being as a passive topic of study and because of the model-driven approach to the development of technology. This approach assumed that it was possible to model the current work activity in formal constructs and from there derive a new technical system that would improve, e.g., information flow and fit nicely into the original organization. Participatory Design was critical to this type of causality and hence to many models used in systems development at the time, e.g., the models of Jackson (1983) and Yourdon (1994).

Participatory Design has strong connections to other parts of the second wave of HCI including the surge of ethnographic and ethnomethodological methods introduced into HCI by, first, Suchman (1987) and, later, the many ethnomethodological studies presented in CSCW research. Both the Participatory Design and the ethnomethodological methods helped researchers and designers raise the criticism of formal models and focus on skillful human beings acting in specific contexts and activities, together. Through the introduction of Lave and Wenger's (1991) notion of communities of practice, for example, notions of learning and human joint development were put in focus.

In this way, Participatory Design had a strong impact on both methods used in practical design of information technology and on reshaping the research field of HCI. At the same time, this also led to Participatory Design becoming synonymous with more basic forms of user-centered design, concentrating on local issues of usability and user satisfaction.

During this time, several parallel ways of dealing with user-centered design developed. Contextual Design was developed by Karen Holtzblatt and others. It was driven by a learning/ partnership model, focusing on the designer as a learner of the use context and as the one making the design decisions. The methods and models of Contextual Design (Holtzblatt and Beyer, 1997) have been promoted and were widespread to design/development organizations across the Western world and are today a part of the standard curriculum of Interaction Design (e.g., Benyon, 2013). Co-design is an approach connected with the increasing involvement of the (industrial) design community in HCI (Sanders and Stappers, 2008). Co-design, to this day, has strong parallels and equally strong differences to Participatory Design. Batya Friedman and colleagues developed their idea of value-sensitive design motivated by a focus on values (Friedman et al., 2017). This focus is somewhat different from the more power- and resource-based analyses of Participatory Design.

As a continuation of the TCO label, the Swedish LO (Swedish Trade Union Confederation), the TCO, and a group of researchers from Swedish universities started the UsersAward (UA) program in 1998. The UsersAward program intended to focus on the involvement of users in IT development. The program worked through domain-specific user surveys and software certifications, as well as prize competitions and led to an increased focus on how users also need to participate in the procurement, deployment, periodic screenings, and further development of the software (Walldius et al., 2015).

The strong commitments in this period developed mainly in terms of more methods and more detailed insights. This era was dominated by methods to make the designers and researchers gain better insight into the use situations and the contexts in which they are embedded. In some ways the move out of Scandinavia came at a price for the original commitments of Participatory Design and our strong commitments in particular. The focus on skill and resources as well as that of focusing on actual human use was in focus and the argument for introducing Participatory Design in North America, whereas the focus on mutual learning and giving back to the users was less on the agenda.

## 3.3    ERA 3: MULTIPLICITY OF METHOD AND FOCI (1998–2013)

The third development that we look at took its starting point in the development of the Participatory Design conferences in the late 1990s and the 2000s, as the research community expanded its reach. The conferences in those years took many steps to open up the field and invite many forms of practitioners and research from many fields. The 2002 conference *"invited researchers, designers and other practitioners to present inquiries into the politics, contexts and practices of collaborative design work"* (Binder et al., 2002, p. ix). Contributions were solicited from a wide array of design fields from fine arts to architecture, urban planning, engineering, and Interaction Design. The 2004 conference further called for contributions across many theoretical traditions, motivated by *"a diverse collection of principles and practices aimed at making technologies and social institutions more responsive to human needs"* (Clement and van den Besselaar, 2004). This introduction defined Participatory Design as the *"direct involvement of people in the codesign of the systems they use,"* essentially pointing away from the political level and negotiation aspects of Participatory Design. The framing of these conferences evidently talked to a wider understanding of design than both the first and second era where information technology was in focus. This has parallels also in the ACM CHI conferences where the topic and focus on "Design" were established.

The many cases and examples found in the proceedings of the Participatory Design Conference in the 2010s are motivated by (user's personal) experience and to some extent politics as personal, etc. instead of the collective resources known from the past. This means an increased focus on what individual users like and do not like, instead of a focus on alternatives that may change the (collective) activities of people and require, e.g., new strategies or new forms of education. Also, both the architectural and the artistic footprint was setting the designer in the center in a manner different from the past, where people are involved as inspiration for designers, rather than the other way around. This focus on personal experience had parallels to HCI in general where also the use contexts and application types broadened, and intermixed, relative to the second wave's focus on work. Research challenged the values related to technology in the second wave (e.g., efficiency) and embraced experience and meaning-making. Hence, methods from Participatory Design were questioned due to the perception that they were dealing only with existing (work) practices and not with emergent use, but many researchers were also trying to extend Participatory Design beyond the workplace.

Many cases engaged users, citizens, or small communities had interesting (personal or experience-based) challenges. A broadened array of papers focused on direct engagements between researchers, designers, and users in different contexts, and expanded discussions of theory and methods into many directions and disciplines. The motivation for researchers and designers of working directly with users' experiences and aspirations was setting the scene for researchers and designers to invent ways of "doing good" for and with people.

An interesting outcome of this era was the *Handbook of Participatory Design* (Simonsen and Robertson, 2012). The chapters of this book were written by configurations of authors central to the research community from mainly Europe, the United States, and Australia, compiling methods and providing a vast overview of the (somewhat fragmented or multidisciplinary) field of that era.

At this time, "participation" became increasingly popular across industry and public administration as a way to better connect to customers and publics. Participatory cultures, sharing economy, social innovation through public engagement, citizen involvement projects, and labs were used to promote civic engagement with technological innovation. Participation was applied across research and industry under a diversity of headlines from Participatory Design, co-design, and co-creation to cooperative design and design thinking.

Ultimately, the ongoing diffusion of participation, design, and computing of this era called for critical reflections in the research community on the core democratic values, politics, and future forms of Participatory Design. This was because political attention and focus on approaches to establish mutual learning was at much weaker intensity, while complemented by pragmatic and ethical arguments for involving users in design.

In summary, this era was characterized by multiplicity in motivation, research paradigm, domains of application, and stakeholders, as well as method. The direct engagement between users and designers/researchers was in focus and hence the strong commitment to skill and resources. However, the political partnerships that are essential to Participatory Design according to our strong commitments were somewhat forgotten or downplayed.

## 3.4    ERA 4: REACHING OUT AND REGAINING POLITICAL TEETH (2014– )

Due to this multiplicity, there was an emerging need for a research agenda that would put politics back in its place. This vacuum was further increased as computer users worldwide seemed to have lost rights in the lights of big transnational corporations. This raised questions about how well Participatory Design scales, from small local interventions to more global concerns. Finally, the vacuum raised concerns for the future of Participatory Design itself, and called for younger activists and researchers to show new directions (see also Smith et al., 2017). These challenges both pointed inward to a scrutiny and modernization of the classical virtues of Participatory Design and outward to different forms of democracy, and to rethinking democracy, to inclusion of new methods, and to addressing new forms of work, and different communities outside work, in various cultures (Bannon et al., 2018a).

The challenge of the big transnationals consisted of two elements: The first was the ways in which local development of technology, e.g., for local government was given up for buying solutions from big transnational corporations, hindering local influence and choice while also often sending national and regional money out of the country to unknown tax havens. Bødker and Kyng (2018) proposed local, open-source development as something that could give some of this control back, but this kind of thinking still has a long way to go. The second was how Facebook, Google, and others offered easily shareable solutions for people at large "for free" whereas it has become very evident to many in recent times that this is not for free at all, and that we all, our communities, and our children at school, pay with our data in ways that are entirely outside our personal, community and even democratic control.

Chapter 4 gives several examples of the kinds of new use contexts and cultures where Participatory Design currently seems to have the potential for change in terms of new methods, new forms of work, and resetting in different cultures. This chapter, however, also points to the importance of interconnected technology use both inside and outside work.

Smith et al. (2017) critically addressed the need for sustained reflection and development of new perspectives on values, characteristics, politics, and future forms of Participatory Design. Interesting newer projects that engage with utilizing and reshaping Participatory Design include Commonfare, Case 3, a European project that has engaged with (young) people in poorer parts of Europe where work is precarious and where as such engaging with technological possibilities and challenges is a way for people to take control over their own lives. This project has engaged with technology across (often lose) work contexts and everyday life for the underprivileged, and suggested a number of ways to reconsider Participatory Design both philosophically and methodologically, not least of which includes considering new ways of involving these underprivileged groups across national and linguistic barriers. In general, the gig, platform, and sharing economy[1] have opened up for new possibilities and challenges with its rhetoric of open and malleable platforms on the one hand, and its focus mainly on establishing commercial success on the other. Participatory Design can be seen as being challenged by, but also having something to offer, to *development of digitally-mediated technologies that value social cooperation as a common good rather than as a source of revenue and accumulation*" (Lyle et al., 2017, p. 256).

Importantly, the critical discussions concerning the Westernized origins and epistemologies of Participatory Design and their ability to travel were addressed through the first Participatory De-

---

[1]  http://sharingandcaring.eu/.

sign Conference in the Global South (apart from Australia) held in Windhoek, Namibia in 2014. The conference engaged a wider local community, NGOs, artists, educators, critics, and politicians alike, and brought about reflections and opportunities for rethinking relations between the Participatory Design community, and practitioners and researchers in the rest of the world.

This was followed by a series of initiatives such as AfriCHI, ArabCHI, and global expansions of a predominantly Western HCI community to Asia and the global south (Szaniecki et al., 2020). Such local initiatives and expandatory efforts of decolonizing HCI research have addressed critical questions for Participatory Design (Smith et al., 2021). To decolonialize in this context means to critically unveil the disguise as inclusive and emancipatory development when this is not the case (Winschiers and Bidwell, 2013). However, these ways of critical questioning have made possible contributions of previously marginalized research communities that are usually subjects of research rather than recognized as active collaborators in, or drivers of, HCI research. The 2020 Participatory Design Conference, held in Manizales, Columbia, strengthened this focus on plurality of voices and empowerment of/in the Global South further, connecting the legacies (of, e.g., Freire) and history of local communities to Western(ized) perspectives and epistemologies.

In summary, this era reaches out in a different manner than the last. With motivation of the need for technological alternatives both locally and worldwide, it raises interesting questions of social value and social goods and reiterates our commitment to democracy, in wider forms. Empowerment of people in this era has been cast more extensively in areas outside formal organizations and pointed at new forms of emancipatory practices. Accordingly, this era has also been focusing on a wider set of future practices.

**Case 3: Commonfare**

Commonfare (commonfare.net) was a recent European project to promote and facilitate new forms of social welfare across vulnerable and less resourceful, precarious groups, e.g., unemployed youth, precarious workers, non-Western migrants, and freelancers. Commonfare was funded from the European Union's Horizon 2020 Research and Innovation Program for the period of 2016–2019. Commonfare has been seeking to establish good practices for, e.g., *"ethical purchasing groups, free software communities, co-housing groups, self-revitalization projects of old abandoned buildings, Fab Labs, co-working spaces and time banks, urban vegetable gardens, community-based and self-organized gyms, mutual aid practices, and networks of artists and freelancers"* (commonfare.net). In doing so, the project pursued new forms of social collaboration starting from local needs and desires.

The project did its activities mainly in three countries. It designed a digital platform to connect people and initiatives across Europe. This software platform (commonfare.net) was to inform people about public measures contrasting poverty, share good practices, and support networking activities that would bring use-value or direct income to people's everyday life (Lyle et al., 2017).

As examples of this platform, the project was seeking to rethink and redesign reputation systems known from many online platforms, so as to avoid stigmatizing people through other people's reviews. Instead, the project developed an algorithmic approach that focused on how people contribute to their network, in terms of who and how many they connected with.

Similarly, Commonfare developed a currency to support their idea of a basic income scheme for all. To avoid collision with, e.g., social welfare payment, it was decided that this currency cannot be exchanged with other currencies, and instead it was made possible to set up currencies for local use, and the currency was tried out in a couple of festivals that Commonfare hosted for their partners.

The project used and developed Participatory Design practices to promote alternatives to digital, commercial platforms of many kinds, such as the above examples. Lyle et al. (2017) discusses how it became important to move beyond working with users' needs, to the recognition of participants' common values (see also Bassetti et al., 2019; Sciannamblo et al., 2018), in their particular case dignity, freedom, autonomy, and self-authorship, as is also reflected, e.g., in the concern for stigmatization mentioned. Lyle et al. (2017) address dignity and autonomy of individuals and their communities as mutual empowerment.

The approach to the design of commonfare.net was *"co-designing and re-imagining ongoing future societal relations based on sustainable and democratic values."* This process addressed various ways in which designers and design researchers could get involved together with institutional actors, such as local governments and grassroots communities at the same time, and in particular in articulating open conflicts between different stakeholders that contribute to the same project. Engaging with different types of institutions and stakeholders at the grassroot level is very dynamic; the needs change and tensions occur at different times, and it was a challenge to adapt the processes, and find a language and vocabulary that works to embrace the tensions, e.g., of how poverty is talked about by governments and institutions and by people themselves. These settings, hence, also challenge who the designers want to side with and even who they can side with, given their own organizational backgrounds.

## 3.5    SUMMARY

We introduced this chapter by asking "How can we learn from the history of Participatory Design?" and pointed to our four strong commitments. In this chapter, we have provided an overview of how Participatory Design has developed from its start until today. The four eras introduced in this chapter provide the background needed for understanding the four commitments. This overview also points out that the commitments, for us as Participatory Design researchers, are embedded in the early projects, and that the middle eras have added nuances, but also that Participatory Design in these eras may appear weaker and somewhat too inclusive.

The four eras expose how Participatory Design has managed to impact many different societal challenges ranging from highly political engagements with trade unions in Scandinavia, over regional creative commons in Southern Europe, to global challenges of postcolonialism and cross-cultural participatory knowledge production. Despite the changing circumstances, scales, and geographical and demographical diversity of Participatory Design, the past 40 years have demonstrated that engaging people in the design process (and decision-making) around computer technology leads to different and more sustainable solutions to societal challenges. This is due to the fact that only people have the power to unleash the potentials in emerging technologies and create the changes we need. The Participatory Design process is the process of unleashing the potentialities of novel technologies in the mutual learning between people and designers. This is why Participatory Design is a very valuable approach when it comes to creating sustainable societal changes based on active engagement of people in the design process.

**Read More**

In this chapter we have provided an overview of the four eras of Participatory Design. However, there is indeed not one canonical history of the field, and this book tells the story from the tradition we have been involved in at Aarhus University. Hence, the history probably looks different depending on where you come from, both geographically, societally, and in terms of your background field. Consequently, we find it suitable to provide additional readings to consult if you want to dive deeper into the multiplicity of the Participatory Design legacy.

**From the early years**

In 1982, a conference in Riva del Sole, Italy gathered researchers and union activists to share experiences from across the Western world, under the auspices of the, otherwise quite mainstream, IFIP (the International Organization of Information Processing) (Briefs et al., 1982). This conference provided a bridge also between the Scandinavian Participatory Design tradition, the British Tavistock tradition of sociotechnical informatics, German research, and international research in the upcoming field of Information Systems (Lanzarra, 2009).

The two first decennial Aarhus conferences (1975 and 1985) at Aarhus University, Denmark, nicely bracketed the early era and illustrated the development that we discuss. The 1975 conference was held in the Nordic languages and gathered many interested researchers and union representatives. The 1985 conference was held in English in order to be more agenda setting and inclusive in terms of many international research agendas dealing in various forms with technology and democracy in the workplace (Bjerknes et al., 1987). The format, however, picked up from the research projects and included thematic working groups that spend time together throughout the conference. In terms of scientific content, one of the working groups produced an inspiring discussion of the (then also) upcoming field of Artificial Intelligence (SAFE Expert Systems, 1987) and the book published from the conference included important contributions starting the theoretical reflections of the Utopia projects (Ehn and Kyng, 1987; Bødker et al., 1987) as well as still surprisingly fresh reflections on design processes and prototyping by Floyd (1987). Bødker's and Ehn's respective books give a deeper theoretical grounding, e.g., to the results of the Utopia project (Bødker, 1990; Ehn, 1988).

A collaboration between Aarhus University and Xerox PARC/Rank Xerox EuroPARC led to the publication of the *Design at Work* book (Greenbaum and Kyng, 1991) that focused more instrumentally on methods to be used by developers/designers with users.

## Participatory Design is Maturing

Proceedings from the Participatory Design Conference from the 1990s and 2000s, as well as the proceedings from the 1995 (Kyng and Mathiassen, 1997) and 2005 (Bertelsen et al., 2005) Aarhus Conferences to some extent, bought into the multiplicity of more experience-based philosophical stances but also provided a more profound focus on interdisciplinarity emphasizing intervention and scholarly critical practice. An interesting outcome of this era was the *Handbook of Participatory Design* (Simonsen and Robertson, 2012). The book consists of 11 co-authored chapters and aims to be a reference book. It frames Participatory Design as being "*about the direct involvement of people in the co-design of the technologies they use*" (ibid, p.X) and addresses the collaborative design processes "driven by the participation of the people affected by the technology designed" (ibid, p.X) The book was the first collective introduction to the field of Participatory Design since the seminal/agenda-setting *Design at Work* (Greenbaum and Kyng, 1991) introduction a decade earlier, and set out to embrace *"a diverse collection of principles and practices aimed at making tech-nologies, tools, environments, businesses, and social institutions more responsive to human needs."*

### The Revitalization of Politics in Participatory Design

The state of Participatory Design was heavily debated in the latter part of the 2010s. Bannon et al., (2018a and b) point to discussions especially at the 2015 Aarhus Conference (Bertelsen et al., 2015) and the Participatory Design Conference 2016 (Bossen et al., 2016b) in Aarhus, Denmark as being important. These discussions led to the articulation of several themes for the call for Bannon et al.'s special issue of ToCHI (Bannon et al., 2018a) including *"a sense that Participatory Design has lost some of its clarity and lacks polit-ical teeth."* This issue, as well as other contributions around that time, included concerns for how the original assumptions of Scandinavian Participatory Design apply in the rest of the world, and even in Scandinavia today: that computer users worldwide have lost rights in light of big transnational corporations; and questions about how well Partici-patory Design scale, from small local interventions to more global concerns. Finally, they raise concerns for the future of Participatory Design, and call for younger activists and researchers to show new directions (see also Smith et al., 2017). The ToCHI special issue (Bannon et al., 2018a) points both inward to a scrutiny and modernization of the classical virtues of Participatory Design and outward to different forms of democracy, as well as rethinking democracy, to inclusion of new methods, and to addressing new forms of work, and different communities outside work, in various cultures.

This expansion to other regions prompted theoretical discussions of postcolonialism (Manisah and Morrison, 2014; Smith et al., 2021; Salazar and Huybrechts, 2020), local-ized, and cross-cultural modes of participatory knowledge production (Winschiers and Bidwell 2013; Winschiers et al., 2017).

# CHAPTER 4

# When and Where Is Participatory Design Done?

Where the previous chapters outlined the main principles of Participatory Design (Chapter 2) and their history (Chapter 3), this chapter addresses the question of where and when Participatory Design is used. There is no algorithm to determine whether or not Participatory Design is applicable in a given situation or in response to a given design problem. As an approach to design, Participatory Design can be applied to any design situation, at least in principle. However, Participatory Design shapes the way design is performed and the way in which the problem is addressed. In this chapter we will provide five examples of arenas in which considerable amounts of Participatory Design work has been done. This is not to suggest that these arenas and problems are particularly amenable to Participatory Design, but to demonstrate how Participatory Design can look when it plays out in different kinds of domains and contexts.

In this chapter you will find:

- a demonstration of the principles of skillfulness, emancipation, democracy, and mutual learning in different domains;

- a resource of Participatory Design literature within different domains; and

- a thematic history of Participatory Design engagement with different domains.

For this chapter we have chosen five domains. They show the breadth of application of Participatory Design and illustrate topics that are central to it. Also, we have chosen domains that are hopefully recognizable if not familiar to students of HCI. This is in order to better demonstrate what is distinct in a Participatory Design approach. The domains are: healthcare; cultural heritage; children and education; government and public services; and communities and publics.

## 4.1 HEALTHCARE

Participatory Design started with a strong focus on work, in classical industries, offices, and production. While early Scandinavian work was closely tied to unions, researchers have, through the years, shared reports on Participatory Design in a wealth of forms and across industries. One of the long-standing domains of Participatory Design engagement is healthcare, starting with the Florence project that was a parallel to Utopia, Case 2, historically (Bjerknes and Bratteteig, 1987). Florence was initially set up to shift the focus from classical men's/blue-collar work to domains dominated by women, in this case nurses, and their forms of knowledge. Nursing was chosen because it is a profession that interacts with other professions. It is dominated by women doing reproduction, service, and information work, in contrast to the more production-oriented forms of labor in Utopia and the early Participatory Design projects.

In later projects, Participatory Design researchers have dealt with issues from the introduction of electronic patient records (Bossen, 2006; Reidl et al., 2008) to ICU (Intensive Care Unit) care (Björgvinsson and Hillgren, 2004), health information systems (Braa et al., 2004), and video consultations (Klammer et al., 2010). Among the most elaborate uses of Participatory Design in healthcare is the work of Hertzum and Simonsen (2010), who worked extensively with patient record systems and handover, coordination, and knowledge sharing in hospital wards.

The Palcom project had a more explicit focus on patients also, e.g., the home treatment of pregnant diabetic patients (Enquist et al., 2007), elderly people (Ballegaard et al., 2008), and emergency medical services (Kyng et al., 2006). In these cases the settings away from the physical framing of the hospital posed challenges to both the treatment of patients, the involvement of the patients, and to the setting of the Participatory Design process as such. Chronically ill patients, e.g., were participating on their own time, and their participation was further complicated by having "good" and "bad" days (Grönvall and Kyng, 2011).

Many of the concerns of the Palcom project led to the 4S project, Case 4: 4S illustrates how open source technologies may become a useful vehicle for local engagement, playing a role in increased democratic control, potentially being a broker for bridging local and national levels of participation, and network activities.

Bødker and Kyng (2018) emphasized the need to do Participatory Design beyond local initiatives and discuss one further health case, HISP, a global network of people, entities, and organizations that design, implement, and sustain Health Information Systems in support of decentralized and empowering structures (Braa and Sahay, 2012). HISP began as an initiative in South Africa to contribute to the provision of useful health-related data on all citizens and to help build flexible local data processing capabilities to support both centrally requested health data, and local effect of health initiatives in the community. HISP represents a long-term perspective with an explicit democracy agenda with a focus on strengthening possibilities for local action and on internationalization based on a growing network of quite different national nodes.

Case 4 and many of the other healthcare cases share a strong concern for the participation of patients as well as the worklife and participation of health professionals, whether in specialized hospital wards, in outpatient clinics or the home. The healthcare area hence is a particularly challenge because it often balances many levels of national and organizational politics (including hospital funding, international health standards, and large international software providers), procedures, skill, collaboration, and daily routines of different groups of health professionals, with the everyday life of patients who may suffer long-term chronic conditions, while generally have most of their lives and activities outside the healthcare setting. Participatory Design in this domain is hence characterized by attempts to bridge many levels of concerns, and the very different conditions of healthcare workers and patients, as also demonstrated in Case 4. Many of the healthcare cases hence show a wider commitment to formal and informal democracy and empowerment of multiple groups of users that are not all part of formal organizations. With such multiplicity comes also tensions between involved groups of participants, and a multiplicity of settings where learning happens, mutually across designers and specific groups of users, but also in processes of mutual learning across groups of users.

**Case 4: 4S**

The 4S case is one of several projects in the healthcare domain, a domain that is interesting since it is dealing with professional users as well as groups of patients, and most often with technologies and examples that unfold over time. The 4S Foundation for Software-based Health Services was set-up to govern open-source software for telemedicine in Denmark (Bødker and Kyng, 2018). The software was mainly developed in Participatory Design projects funded by different public research and development grants. 4S was established in 2013 to govern a focus on OpenTele and an infrastructure toolbox of collection of open-source software, among other elements. However, in the process of setting this up, 4S has moved toward cooperation between healthcare personnel and researchers/activists, and hence toward more and more emphasis on workplace democracy.

4S has been driven by researchers in Participatory Design, IT managers from the public hospital sector, doctors and other healthcare personnel working at public hospitals, in addition to members of patient organizations (Kyng, 2015). Patients/citizens and healthcare personnel are groups that experience major changes affecting their daily life or work when telehealth is introduced. There are, however, very asymmetric power relations in this field, both internally in the hospital sector and when it comes to patients, who often lack networks and other resources. This has been a major concern regarding representation in the project.

OpenTele was designed as a series of Participatory Design activities rooted in ongoing use. The developed software was used to demonstrate implications of the vision and to engage personnel and patients in these processes (Bødker and Kyng, 2018). This initiative has illustrated the importance of working at different levels of public government, while combining arguments, based in different professions and activities, and developing software that is open and accessible.

The 4S software ecosystem (Christensen et al., 2014) was set up to support these processes by providing reusable components and services that incorporate national and international standards and increase integration and interoperability through components that access national services in interoperable ways.

In developing the open software infrastructure, 4S became a successful mechanism for sustaining democratic user influence by *"facilitating and sustaining direct influence on the use and development of telehealth by healthcare professionals, patients and citizens"* (Kyng 2015).

4S is hence an example of a Participatory Design case that is concerned with politics and ways of influencing decisions at national and local scales, while involving both professional and citizen users along with decision makers. 4S is also an important case for the development of open software platforms and the democratic mechanisms around them.

## 4.2    CULTURAL HERITAGE

How do we combine the past with the contemporary to engage people in cultural heritage communication? During the past two decades, Participatory Design has increasingly impacted the way we approach exhibition spaces and the audience experience in which an emphasis is put on extending established museum design practices (Taxén, 2004). Most notably, Simon's work on The participatory Museum (Simon, 2010) emphasized the importance of an *audience-centered* approach to cultural heritage communication, the idea that visitors *construct their own meaning* from cultural experiences and that audiences' voices can inform and invigorate exhibition spaces. With a participatory mindset, the cultural institutions are transitioned into a place where visitors can create, share and connect with each other around content. Here, the content of the exhibition was no longer seen as the center of the experience. Rather, the mutual learning process emerging between people in the audience and with the curators through the construction of the exhibition space became central to the museum experience.

Similarly, Iversen and Smith (2012) described the participatory design process leading to a future exhibition through processes of "dialogical curation" between curators, experts, designers, and audiences. Here, the process of participation was rooted in the design of the cultural heritage content and prolonged into the exhibition by means of engaging elements by which audiences could access, modify, co-curate, and add to the existing exhibition space. They emphasized that innovations in digital cultural communication for museums provided new challenges regarding the development of appropriate methods for participation in curatorial processes, hence calling for re-thinking the role of audiences in exhibitions (Smith and Iversen, 2014). The Digital Natives project, Case 7, focuses specifically on teenagers as participants in cultural exhibitions.

Recent studies do not only evolve around the exhibition space or the curation process, but also around processes of decolonizing Participatory Design research (Smith et al., 2020a). Here political matters such as unrevealing the collective memory of suppressed cultural heritage is recovered through participatory design processes. Through participatory engagement with Namibian youth, Kambunga et al. (2020) argued that exploring young people's everyday colonial experiences in and past alternative narratives present an opportunity to contribute to the process of decoloniality, whereby the youth's voices become part of collective consciousness and commemoration when it comes to colonial memories. In their understanding of cultural heritage and "the past", these are "subjective, fluid, and constantly renegotiated" in processes of engagement and participation. Case 5 describes a number of attempts to work with indigenous tribes on their cultural heritage, through Participatory Design. Here, Participatory Design in cultural heritage has become a process of owning and reinterpreting the past to better understand and take ownership of the present and future (Kambunga et al., 2020).

### Case 5: Preserving Cultural Heritage Across Indigenous Tribes

Winschiers and colleagues, as an important case of cultural heritage projects, have worked long term with technology design for and with indigenous communities in Namibia (Winschiers-Theophilus and Bidwell, 2013, Winschiers-Theophilus et al., 2017). The researchers emphasized the success of a Participatory Design process is dependent on both the individual participants' commitment and engagement, as well as on the collective communities' agendas and cohesion (Kapuire et al., 2015). Their work critiques generalized forms of community participation and ways of "being participated" by research teams (Winschiers-Theophilus et al., 2010). As community technology design is directly impacted by dominant discourses in community development, HCI, and design, applying different cultural lenses shift not only practices but also directs the levels of awareness, thereby unfolding fundamentally distinct cultural engagement approaches (Winschiers-Theophilus et al., 2017). Hence, the authors' address central issues of marginalized voices and how developers model "users" across cultures and reinforce their own bias in technology design.

With interdisciplinary research teams, the authors created a number of diverse projects connected to the Indigenous Knowledge Technologies research cluster at Namibia University of Science and Technology (NUST). Over time, teams included young members of the indigenous OvaHerero and OvaHimba tribe themselves, but also village elders who showed interest in the technology and the project aiming at preserving their cultural heritage.

The OvaHimba tribe consists of nomadic cattle farmers that move around from one location to the next searching for better grazing land for their livestock. The number of oxen one owns is seen as a sign of wealth, fame, and respect in the community. The OvaHimba is one of the tribes in Namibia that have maintained their cultural customs, and are rich in indigenous knowledge, which the authors worked with around their productive grazing system.

The researchers worked across several tribal groups to identify and select relevant real-world items to be modeled and found that often participants knew exactly what they wanted and readily engaged in the process, e.g., taking photos for the 3D graphic designers (Stanley et al., 2015). Participants urged the researchers' engagement with the community and over time built close relationships with particular members of the community.

In a collaboration with the Erindi-Roukambe community in Eastern Namibia, Rodil et al. (2012) co-designed and developed a tablet-based 3D visualization preservation tool for indigenous knowledge called the Home Stead Creator (HSC). The HSC allowed users to build their homesteads and create scenarios of cultural practices by dragging and dropping 3D traditional objects, representing real elements, in the rural surroundings to be placed on a soil look-alike surface. The Home Stead Creator was evaluated across OvaHerero and Ova-Himba communities and traditions, comparing, e.g., different cultural representations of huts, fences, and people's attires. The OvaHimba elders expressed that the "OvaHerero version" of the HSC would not serve the purpose of preserving OvaHimba cultural heritage, which was a confirmation that the 3D models needed to be replaced with models that adequately represented the OvaHimba traditions. Being part of the national digitization effort of Namibian Indigenous Knowledge, the researchers addressed how they could speed up ethnical adaptations of the system, more specifically the fast production of these 3D graphic models even for other rural communities.

With the aim to create locally appropriate technology within a cross-cultural paradigm, the researchers engaged the community to validate not only the developed technology but the models used as a basis of design as well as ongoing cultural interpretations. This responsibility of the researchers demands skills that are often not taught as part of the computer science curricula, such as increased awareness of the context in which the model, interpretation, and translation takes place, which only evolve through engagement over time.

Acknowledging that each engagement is built on different premises, the authors suggested that the approach to cultural engagement is a conscious choice, which frames the interactions and outcomes of the community collaboration within participation and empowerment. Thus, a radical paradigm shift was suggested for research and development work, embracing a blending of epistemologies, recognizing contributions from all participants, including the designers, within a collective context. A transcultural approach to community technology development is promoted, to strive for awareness, which needs to be cultivated over time among participants within the design space (Winschiers-Theophilus et al., 2017).

Participatory Design regarding cultural heritage takes many forms. It involves both professional curators, and everyday people both as, e.g., museum visitors and members of the cultures being curated and dealt with in various forms. In much of the literature in this field, Participatory Design methods are used and developed with challenges similar to, e.g., government and public services (below) but, as Case 5 indicates, some of the research regarding cultural heritage have also led to forms of radical rethinking of assumptions and methods of Participatory Design, including commitments to democracy, empowerment, emancipation, and resources.

## 4.3    CHILDREN AND EDUCATION

Do children have a voice in the design of their everyday technologies? If children are the experts of their everyday life, why are these experts not involved in the design process? These crucial questions surfaced in the beginning of the new millennium in the work of Druin (1999), Read et al. (2002), and Iversen (2005). By using Participatory Design, children were admitted to the design process due to dedicated Participatory Design methods and techniques to adjust for imbalances in the power relations between researchers and children during design. Methods such as Kidsreporter (Bekker et al., 2003), Cooperative inquiry (Druin, 1999), Bluebells (Kelly et al., 2006), and Fictional Inquiry (Iversen and Dindler, 2008) gained popularity within the emerging area of child–computer interaction as ways in which children were able to express their needs and wants in the development of future technologies. The ultimate end goal of these processes was to empower children to have a strong voice in the development of their future technologies.

However, as Participatory Design methods became mainstream over the past 20 years, Read et al. (2016) raised concern for the ethical aspects of engaging children in Participatory Design work that they proposed had become too "fast and furious," also described as "reduced Participatory Design." Two challenges emerge. First, if an emphasis is put on simply collecting children's novel ideas for new technology design, the strong Participatory Design commitment of empowering users through design would fail. Second, if the Participatory Design process involving children is conducted to produce results describing how children liked a certain design concept, a Participatory Design workshop or the company of adult researchers, the Participatory Design aspect would be reduced to no more than do-gooding. In both cases, the strong commitment of participatory design (as described in Chapter 2) would fail. To reconnect to the Participatory Design commitments, Iversen et al. (2017) emphasized the educational aspects of Participatory Design with children.

In their protagonist approach to designing with children, Iversen et al. (2017) revitalized Participatory Design's ideal of the design process as an education activity. In this approach children were engaged to learn how to design their own technologies and take an active stance regarding emerging technologies. This resonated with Bødker (2003) who proposed that designers or researchers should work with people, groups or organizations to explore what current and future technologies may support them in their particular setting. The idea was not so much to build specific future technology as it was to help people realize that they have a choice. Today, Child–Computer Interaction is an increasingly important research area for developing Participatory Design methods, techniques, and practices. Research results related to what has been called the third space of Participatory Design, the space between design and use (Makhaeva et al., 2016), the sustainability of participatory practices (Smith and Iversen, 2018), the accountability and rigor of Participatory Design practice (Frauenberger et al., 2015), and the micro-ethics of participatory design (Spiel et al., 2018) all derive from Participatory Design research conducted with children.

Participatory Design with children is special because it includes special concerns regarding methods, representativity, and, e.g., ethics for engaging with children and educating children for democracy. Case 6 illustrates how Participatory Design with children is also much more than that because it reaches out to both the skills and empowerment of teachers, to emancipation in unevenly balanced power relations between teachers and children, to future technologies that are more directly relevant to some teachers than students, and to many levels of decision makers in school management, school boards, and local and national politics.

### Case 6: FabLab@School.dk

The FabLab@School.dk project is one example of projects in the domain of children and education. The project was launched based on a 2014 reform of standards in the Danish primary and lower secondary school, emphasizing the use of digital technology and a strong focus on competencies related to "21st century skills" (Ananiadoui and Claro, 2009). This new educational reform emphasized the use of digital technology in all subject areas, and a new craft and design program replaced woodwork and needlework to support the innovative and entrepreneurial competences of future generations. In response to this increased focus on IT in education, a small group of interdisciplinary researchers at Aarhus University, together with the three Danish municipalities, initiated a three-year project, FabLab@School.dk, to develop and sustain digital fabrication and design thinking as parts of lower secondary teaching. The aim was to develop an educational environment that encouraged teachers, students, and schools to integrate new digital fabrication technologies (3D printers, laser cutters, etc.) and digital construction kits (Arduino, Makey-Makey, LillyPads, etc.) into the process of solving real-world problems as part of the educational training. The research explored the central qualities and dynamics of design literacy for students, and how this core competence could be scaffolded through constructive and critical digital design processes (Smith et al., 2015).

The project was based on the global FabLab@School concept developed by the Transformative Technologies Learning Lab at Stanford University, but extended its focus with a distinctly participatory approach. This project did design activities at many organizational levels evolving around technology, decision-making, competence-building, commitment, and policy-making. The organization of the Danish project was unique in terms of its participatory research foundation and the partnership between municipalities and academic research, which allowed for the creation of an extended living lab involving diverse stakeholders of students, teaching staff, local politicians, and international researchers. Digital fabrication in education was novel in the local context and the set-up created the basis for defining a common direction and offered flexibility to develop the research agenda in appropriate ways, as our insights evolved throughout the project (Smith and Iversen, 2018).

The participatory processes played out in several political and practical arenas and the project involved many different types of activities. FabLab@School engaged students and teachers in obtaining long-term perspectives on digital thinking, design, and democracy. It reached across levels of authority of the educational system, and covered the many parents, students, teachers, industry representatives, and policy-makers that took part in participatory design activities throughout and after the project (Bødker et al., 2017).

At the national political level, Participatory Design methods were used to stimulate emerging new configurations of collaborators through activities addressing future infrastructures. Other activities were set up to develop new foundations for a national curriculum for a subject of Technology Comprehension in the Danish school system (Smith et al., 2020b; Dindler et al., 2021). Hence, what was initiated as a regional cross-collaborative initiative, created both a new community of practice spanning several hundreds of schools and stakeholders across municipalities (from students, teachers, to local politicians), as well as a new knowledge foundation for the production of a national curriculum.

### Case 7: Digital Natives

The "Digital Native" project designed engaging museum exhibitions for teenagers (aged 14–16) with an emphasis on digital technologies and collective memory sharing (Iversen and Smith, 2012; Smith and Iversen, 2011, 2014).

Digital Natives (2008–2010) was a research and exhibition experiment exploring the intersections of cultural heritage, Participatory Design, and new interactive technologies. The project experimented with possible new futures of cultural heritage communication, and involved creative collaboration between a group of young people (aged 16–18), anthropologists, and interaction designers through a period of nine months (Smith and Iversen, 2011; Smith, 2013).

The project focused on the contemporary generation of young people raised in the digital era, surrounded by new digital technologies, and whose lives are said to depart from that of previous generations, both mentally, socially, and culturally (Prensky, 2001; Ito, 2009). The exhibition explored digital natives' everyday cultures, identities, and communication practices, and experimented with new ways of representing these cultures in the context of a concrete museum exhibition. As such, the aim of Digital Natives was to create an exhibition in collaboration with a group of young people, which explored the lives and cultures of the digital natives' generation in a specific local setting.

The project was exploratory in nature, actively interweaving boundaries between cultural heritage and contemporary digital cultures. Focusing on issues of participation and interaction, the aim was to create new modes of communication and engagement that would create dialogical spaces and novel connections between museum space, exhibition and audiences. Digital Natives was held at the Aarhus Center for Contemporary Art in December 2010. Five interactive installations were created for the exhibition that focused on the everyday lives and practices of seven young digital natives.

## 4.4    GOVERNMENT AND PUBLIC SERVICES

Participatory design in public sector projects is not new and several early projects were dealing with, e.g., nurses in hospitals and public inspection work, such as labor or building/construction inspection (Trigg and Bødker, 1994; Sperschneider et al., 2003). Participatory Design on the boundary between public sectors and the citizens is a newer phenomenon, partly relating to the use of social technologies/Web 2.0 in this setting. Web 2.0 was celebrated originally for distributing power from central institutions to the masses through involvement but the use of such platforms has been limited in many areas of public government. Pilemalm (2018) discussed e-government initiatives targeting groups of citizens who are supposed to collaborate with the authorities in carrying out certain tasks for themselves and their co-citizens, and talked about this as a we-government or a do-it-yourself government. She mentioned neighborhood watch programs, park clean-ups, healthcare counseling, and emergency response as examples of this. The eGov+ project, Case 8, similarly discussed forms of citizen services such as parental leave planning, ordering of new passports, registration of moving of residence, application of various subsidiaries (Bohøj et al., 2010), and local urban planning (Bohøj et al., 2011). Saad-Sulonen worked with the meeting of Participatory Design with urban planning and end-user development, and proposed two different kinds of Participatory Design in this space, a traditional, staged participatory design, and participation as design-in-use (Saad-Sulonen, 2014).

Based on their eGov+ project, Case 8, Bødker and Zander (2015) discussed the potentials of Participatory Design in the context of municipal government by pointing to some tensions between municipal government as a place to exercise democracy in the development and introduction of technology, and municipal government as a place of work, with its needs and requirements from workers as users and management as in charge of resources, delegation, and planning of work.

### Case 8: eGov+ Municipal Planning

This case is an example of a project on the boundaries of public services and citizen participation. It was about public deliberation in municipal planning exploring the possibilities of location-aware mobile technology. To work with public deliberation in the evaluation of municipal plans via mobile, location-aware technologies, citizens needed to imagine the implications of the municipal plan, an abstract, bureaucratic object. The case is part of the eGov+ project which did participatory design across citizens and municipal governments in different areas of e-governance services and infrastructure (Bohøj et al., 2011).

The eGov+ project worked with participatory design on the boundaries between professional users such as caseworkers and citizens, in this particular case, citizens and municipal planners. Whereas planners are easily identified by employer and professional title, nearly all individuals living in a municipality can be categorized as citizens. The project engaged in a more thorough collaboration with two groups: a local interest group pertaining to a parish and an ad-hoc interest group that had come together due to a particular planning issue regarding expropriation of a piece of land. Moreover, individual citizens of various age groups and backgrounds were involved to counterbalance the very active citizens in the two interest groups.

What was known as the Mobile Democracy case focused on Danish municipal planning, where a new municipal plan is created every 12 years. This plan is continuously revised through a process where the municipality is required by law to encourage and receive input from ministries, public and private institutions, commercial and non-profit organizations, as well as private citizens. The initial focus of the case was the involved municipality's wish for more and better qualified complaints and proposals to municipal plans. The municipality has had little success in mobilizing citizens to participate in the municipal plan revision. Where representatives of the municipality wished to gain a better understanding of citizen involvement, it soon became apparent that the main concern of the involved citizens was to be heard by their municipality.

Mobile Democracy deployed a broad set of design methods including future workshops, extreme scenarios, role-playing games, cultural probes, scenarios, storyboards, paper prototypes, and mock-ups of various kinds (see also Chapter 7). The project constructed role-playing games assigning different roles to citizens asking them to discuss fictive dilemmas, and how such discussions could be supported via mobile technology. Concurrently with the paper prototypes, functional software prototypes for smartphones were developed. With these prototypes the project conducted "walkshops" (Korn and Zander, 2010). All of these contributed to the iterative design process. Prototypes were used as alternative suggestions, providing potential users with the possibility of exploring the issue hands-on (Korn and Bødker, 2012). Moreover, the prototypes served as a way of probing the context of citizen participation in municipal planning.

In addition to Case 8, eGov+, both Cases 4 and 6 illustrate proactive attempts at organizing larger projects to engage with workers from public organizations as well as their organizational and political management. These cases emphasize in various ways the double role of these kinds of workers as also citizens with a democratic voice. And at the same time the cases illustrate the needs and means of engaging both the local level of, e.g., a local school or hospital ward, with their interests and resources, and various more central levels as well as central strategic planners and decision-makers. Case 4 illustrates how these political levels were activated to promote open-source technology as an alternative to investment with large international software corporations. This was done with the argument that resources would hence be under better local democratic control.

These cases (4, 6, 7) show how Participatory Design projects have engaged with many levels of democracy and organization beyond the specific users of a specific technology. They point to a particular concern for how to engage with different levels of democratically controlled organizations, from a do-it-yourself government to national and international organizations, to allow exploration of future practices and alternative technologies and utilize what are essentially alternative business models, where the return of investment would come back to society.

## 4.5    COMMUNITIES AND PUBLICS

Robinson (1991) discussed the co-operative movement and its very long history (from Minoan civilization 5,000 years ago, via the industrial revolution, to the 750,000 co-operative societies in the 1980s). He pointed out how this movement has always had a problem of coordinating disparate viewpoints in a democratic way. Carroll and Rosson (2007) argue for why Participatory Design is particularly important when it comes to local communities where "*the user population is diverse, ranging from young children playing educational games at a museum to elderly shut-in citizens sending email to loved ones.*" In such communities, they argue it is particularly difficult for outsiders to anticipate the needs of the users. In addition, as mentioned also above, the technical artifacts and infrastructure of such communities are diverse and difficult to understand, without direct involvement of households and community building.

The sharing or platform economy has further put an emphasis on the question of how bottom-up communities organize and develop around technologies, be they physically collocated or not. Commonfare, Case 3, is a European project that promotes and facilitates new forms of social welfare across vulnerable and less resourceful, precarious groups, e.g., immigrant workers. In particular, the project uses and develops Participatory Design practices to promote alternatives to the digital, commercial (platform economy) platforms. The project has designed a shared digital platform to support such needs across languages and cultures in Europe, with a basis in Participatory Design.

Participatory Design has shown useful when designing for and with communities. The particular challenges to Participatory Design are how to make use of the resources available in the community while also exploring possible futures. How can we move beyond the immediate needs of users, toward their shared values? What are the particular challenges of siding with more short-term, vulnerable, and precarious groups?

Civics and publics are concepts used to frame activities that happen between people as citizens in local debate, though not necessarily only as citizens in classical politics. Examples may be people who together use apps to understand patterns of bike riding in cities, and to discuss and promote, e.g., location-based services for local, urban planning on the go, or for engaging people in management of disasters. Björkvinsson et al. (2012) use Dewey's idea of publics to address such settings through conflicts and heterogeneity, basically emphasizing that there is no public without something to be against. LeDantec and DiSalvo (2013) address power structures and marginalization. When Participatory Design is applied in these contexts it is important to embrace multiple perspectives and voices, power structures as well as people that are in the center versus others who are peripheral or marginalized in some way or the other.

In this perspective, there are two important challenges to design methods at large and to Participatory Design in particular: How do you do design in ways that take into consideration what holds people together and what they are against? How do you deal with democracy and empowerment both with those who are marginalized (or get marginalized through technology) and those in the center? Case 3 presents an example of many of these concerns, and there are traces of them also in Cases 4, 5, 6, and 8. It is generally the case that Participatory Design picks up the possibility, and the challenges of working with diverse groups of users, but this also creates challenges that are different from how HCI often works to categorize users based on their similarities rather than differences. Hence, it is important to consider what happens on the boundaries of the groups when technology is developed and introduced, and how technology may be used to bring forth multiple voices in constructive controversies when considering the resourceful development of future practices.

## 4.6    WHEN AND WHERE HAS PARTICIPATORY DESIGN BEEN APPLIED?

When Participatory Design is moved from work to more mixed and multiple settings as some of those presented above, it is also dealing with groups of people who are heterogenous in terms of power, resources, and cultures, even more so than in the classical work setting.

Communities, public (who have a joint cause and something to be against), and more organized political contexts often deal with both people who work and represent formal democratic, political, or organizational units and people who participate as citizens or community members, perhaps with certain particular interests. The meeting of formal, organizational structures and development thereof, and the public and communities that are active in the setting as far as their resources go, or until they lose interest, need to be considered in the Participatory Design processes.

These types of settings are characterized by multiplicities of skills, concerns, and technologies, both the multiple, often coming and going technologies, the infrastructuring with existing technologies, and the possible inventions of the people themselves play important parts in the Participatory Design processes. As we pointed out, boundaries between groups and communities are important and need to be considered. Marginalization is an important concern, and even a possible resource for the Participatory Design process. Vulnerable groups of patients, and children as participants at large, are examples of groups that we have put extra focus on in this respect.

Working across cultures such as with ingenious populations or precarious groups across Europe makes it even more important to emphasize a classical Participatory Design lesson that users are not like you. This is indeed also an important reason why it is interesting to see Participatory Design deployed in cultures that are very different from the northern European where it was born, and to confront our strong commitments as we have done here. We will return to examples in later chapters, and we generally encourage our readers to consider projects that take their own local cultures seriously.

## 4.7    SUMMARY

We introduced this chapter by asking "when and where is Participatory Design done?" The chapter illustrates how Participatory Design is a highly context-sensitive approach, applied successfully in many different domains including healthcare, cultural heritage, children and education, and communities and publics. Two main takeaways are provided in the chapter. First, the chapter presents a thematic history of Participatory Design engagement with different domains supported by rich case materials from Participatory Design work by colleagues and ourselves. Each of the domain descriptions accompanied by the cases provides a detailed account of how Participatory Design works differently in different domains. Second, reading across the different Participatory Design encounters in different domains makes it possible to understand the context-sensitive and moldable nature of Participatory Design without compromising its strong commitments. We close the chapter by discussing how Participatory Design also engages with groups of people who are heterogenous in terms of power, resources, and cultures.

**Read More**

Bødker gives a thorough account of the theoretical and methodological development of HCI in Bødker (2006 and 2015). Björkvinsson et al. (2012) use Dewey's idea of public as a frame for addressing such settings through conflicts and heterogeneity. LeDantec and DiSalvo (2013) move on from Dewey to think about power structures and marginalization. When Participatory Design is applied in the public realm it is necessary to consider such issues as context, scale, and ethics (Dalsgaard, 2010; De Angeli et al., 2014), as well as embracing multiple perspectives and voices (Cozza and De Angeli, 2015; Sciannamblo et al., 2018).

Participatory Design in public sector projects is dealt with in several early projects, e.g., nurses in hospitals (Bjerknes and Bratteteig, 1987) and later casework in inspection work (Bødker, 1993; Trigg and Bødker 1994). Participatory Design on the boundary between public sectors and the citizens is a newer phenomenon (Pilemalm, 2018), partly relating to the use of social technologies/Web 2.0 in this setting (see also Bødker and Zander, 2015). The eGov+ project discussed such forms as citizen services and parental leave planning, ordering of new passports, registration of moving of residence, and application of various subsidiaries (Bohøj et al., 2010, 2011).

Healthcare has been in focus in work by Bossen (2006), Reidl et al. (2008), Björgvinsson and Hillgren (2004), Braa et al. (2004), and Klammer et al. (2010). Hertzum and Simonsen (2010) worked extensively with patient record systems and handover, coordination, and knowledge sharing in hospital wards. The Palcom project addressed home treatment of pregnant diabetic patientients (Enquist et al., 2007) and emergency medical services (Kyng et al., 2006); see also Grönvall and Kyng (2011). Braa and Sathay (2012) and Braa et al. (2004) present the HISP project, an international, longitudinal project.

Druin (1999), Read et al. (2002), and Iversen (2005) were among the initiators of Participatory Design with children. Methods were developed such as Kidsreporter (Bekker et al., 2003), Cooperative inquiry (Druin et al., 1999), BlueBell (Kelly et al., 2006), and Fictional Inquiry (Dindler and Iversen, 2007).

Bustamante et al. (2018) discussed Participatory Design in the context of young refugees who found themselves in new cultures, and considered how Participatory Design processes can be set up to support them in these vulnerable conditions. Other works from the literature focused instead on the use and transformation into other cultures outside the Western one (see also Case 5).

In addition to different domains, the Participatory Design Conferences have made attempts to open up to different cultural contexts by hosting conferences in both Africa and South America, and the community is diversifying. Many questions are raised regarding the usefulness and transformation of these new contexts. Having failed to solicit papers from other cultures for their Special Issue of ToCHI, Bannon et al. (2018a) raised concerns regarding the journals and their review processes per se. As seen from the perspective of this book, this generally raises meta-concerns for the appreciation and usefulness of activities and methods across cultural settings.

# PART II

# The Participatory Design Toolbox

CHAPTER 5

# What Are the Activities and Methods of Participatory Design?

In the following three chapters we address Participatory Design from the perspective of practice and methods. We do this by exploring the main activities and methods of Participatory Design in this chapter, the tools and materials in Chapter 6, and the principles of organizing Participatory Design processes, specifically with respect to the collaboration between users and researchers/designers in Chapter 7. Through these chapters we equip readers with a methodological toolbox and a look into the literature on how Participatory Design is conducted.

As with many other design approaches, through the years, PD practitioners have developed particular methods and ways of working that reflect the main concerns of Participatory Design. However, PD practitioners will also typically use methods and tools that are common to other design approaches. To complicate matters, many disciplines, including HCI and Interaction Design, have been inspired by Participatory Design's direct involvement of users and today user involvement in design is found in many areas including parts of industry where designers engage with users as part of the development process. This means that we cannot present a neatly delineated catalog of methods that are unique to Participatory Design. Instead, we start this chapter by outlining how Participatory Design presents itself in practice; that is, the typical activities in which Participatory Design practitioners engage. We use our four strong commitments to point to and understand the purposes that different methods may serve and why some methods are more attuned to the kinds of results that Participatory Design pursues. This also means abandoning the idea that there are PD-specific methods and non-PD methods. Instead, we describe the methods often used and cited in Participatory Design and demonstrate how they are attuned to the purposes of Participatory Design.

Hence, this chapter points to main activities and frequently used methods in Participatory Design. It furthermore highlights how methods have been appropriated and brought into design by use of examples from our own research portfolio. To organize these methods, we will begin by characterizing the kinds of activities that PD practitioners usually engage in.

The two main takeaways of this chapter are:

- Participatory Design can be characterized in terms of five main activities—field studies, workshops, collaborative prototyping, infrastructuring, and evaluation—and

- a collection of methods are used in these main activities.

## 5.1    UNDERSTANDING PARTICIPATORY DESIGN ACTIVITIES

Most HCI textbooks take their starting point with a small number of Interaction Design activities, including the outline of four main activities of Preece et al. (2019) (see Figure 5.1). In order to connect this chapter to well-known practices in HCI and Interaction Design, we begin by considering how the overarching activities of Participatory Design compare to what is typically found in an Interaction Design process, exemplified through Preece et al. (2019). This model iterates between analyses of existing practices to establish requirements, designing to suggest alternatives to meet these requirements, prototyping to build and make ideas available to users, and evaluating to ensure the quality of the design.

| Interaction Design | | Participatory Design | |
|---|---|---|---|
| **Activities** | **Purpose** | **Activities** | **Purpose** |
| Establishing Requirements | Understanding the needs of future users | Field Studies | Understanding practice and initiating mutual learning |
| Designing Alternatives | Suggesting ideas that meet requirements | Workshops | Facilitating the meeting between diverse stakeholders |
| Prototyping | Making tangible representations of design ideas for users to engage with | Collaborative Prototyping | Collaboratively exploring and developing design alternatives |
| Evaluating | Measuring the qualities (e.g., usefulness, usability, etc.) of the designed product | Infrastructuring | Securing that social, organizational, and technical infrastructures are in place to support sustainability of results |
| | | Evaluation | Assessing the outcomes of design |

Figure 5.1: Comparison of main activities in Interaction Design and Participatory Design. To the left, a general user-centered design model (here from Preece et al., 2019) as presented in several textbooks and introductions to design. To the right, our proposed characterization of five central Participatory Design activities.

In the following we present an alternative set of activities that better capture and characterize five central Participatory Design activities (Brodersen Hansen et al., 2019). The proposed structure has strong parallels to the standard model at the same time it emphasizes mutual learning instead of requirements, workshops as the main means of bringing stakeholders together, the active use of prototyping for exploration of the future and hands-on experience with it, and the embedding of the activities as both technical and social infrastructuring. Finally, a somewhat reiterated version of evaluation. In other words, the Participatory Design model has strong ties to our definition of Participatory Design and the four *strong commitments* of *democracy*, at the workplace and beyond; *empowerment* of people through the *processes of design*; the aims for *emancipatory practices* rooted in *mutual learning* between designers and people; and seeing human beings as *skillful* and *resourceful* in the development of their *future practices*.

In the following subsections we present the activities and provide examples of Participatory Design methods that are common with the five activities.

## 5.2    FIELD STUDIES

Field studies may be understood as activities in which primarily qualitative methods are applied to study the current practice, context, and domain of potential future users and stakeholders. Whereas field studies in general include observation, interviews, and video analysis, the focus in Participatory Design is not only on gathering data, but also on collaborative reflection on current practices and initiating mutual engagement. Field studies in Participatory Design are typically the basis for subsequent workshops, prototyping, infrastructuring, and evaluation.

Studying practice and real-life use situations "in the wild" have permeated Participatory Design practice, and ethnographic methods have played a prominent role since the early 1990s (see Greenbaum and Kyng, 1991; Bjerknes and Bratteteig, 1995). Concrete methods like interviews and participant observation were adapted, and the active engagement with users in their contexts was discussed, leading to parallel developments also of the partnership model of Contextual Design (Holtzblatt and Beyer, 1997). In the meeting between U.S.-trained anthropologists and Scandinavian Participatory Design researchers (Greenbaum and Kyng, 1991, Blomberg and Karasti, 2012), the appropriate relation between studying and involving participants in design came to the fore. Based on this, Participatory Design as a field has developed methods for studying the practice and context of potential users, highlighting for instance the use of video for understanding practice (Suchman and Trigg, 1992), contextual design (Holtzblatt and Beyer, 1997), and scenarios as representations of current practice (Carroll, 2000). More recently, the discussion of the role and nature of anthropology and ethnography in Participatory Design has been renewed making the case for a more engaged "design anthropology" focusing on continuous knowledge production and cultural exploration (Smith and Kjærsgaard, 2015; Gunn et al., 2013; Smith et al., 2016).

Field studies are most frequently used to familiarize PD researchers with an existing practice that is the subject for change. This often involves observations or participant observations in which researchers engage with the people and objects that are already engaged in the practice. In the Digital Natives project, Case 7, the field studies included hours of observation in existing museum environments to encounter how teenagers were currently approaching sites of cultural heritage and how they were approached by curators, exhibits, and staff members. In this particular case, the observations were quite simple. With prior authorization from the museum and groups of visiting teenagers (schools), the researchers followed the visitors around the exhibition space, observing, taking notes, and asking questions about their perception of the exhibition space and their motivation for engaging with museum objects. In some cases in which teenagers were actively engaged in the exhibition, they were asked to explain how and why this part of the exhibition seemed more interesting than other parts. In some cases, video was used to record elements of the museum visit. Video recordings were valuable to the extent that they could be analyzed off-site and shared among a team of researchers. Occasionally, teenagers were invited into the design project to co-analyze video data from the field studies or to validate the prior analysis. Field studies were also used to look for possible design openings and to compile now-scenarios (a condensed version of how a typical visit at a museum would be like for a group of teenagers) to communicate the analysis to museum curators, teenagers, and other stakeholders involved.

Sometimes field studies take other forms than observations or participant observations. Digital Natives, Case 7, targeted the understanding of how teenagers would communicate digitally, to explore how museums could utilize digital technologies in and around their exhibition space. An exclusive agreement with five teenagers and their guardians was made to access their digital profiles, text messages, social media profiles, etc. The collection included more than 2,500 postings that were analysed together with the teenagers themselves, to fully understand how and to what extent teenagers would construct knowledge through their social relations. Field studies in this particular case were a mutual learning process in which researchers together with teenagers co-explored the digital landscape of a teen by clustering and tagging the 2,500 items from their smartphones (see Figure 5.2). In that way, field studies were used to incorporate elements of workshops that are presented in the following section.

Generally, field studies emphasize how people at large, and users in particular, are skillful and resourceful in their everyday practices and activities and are set up to help mutual learning between users and researchers/designers. Generally, field studies look toward current practices more than the future, even though future possibilities may also be addressed through collaborative and design-driven field study methods (see Smith et al., 2016; Blomberg and Karasti, 2012).

Figure 5.2: A teenager in the Digital Natives project with her collection of smartphone pictures and printed messenger statements, organized through collaborative field research to better understand the teenagers' online presence.

## 5.3    WORKSHOPS

The workshop is often portrayed as the hallmark activity of Participatory Design—the scene of direct collaboration between designers, researchers, computer professionals, future users, and stakeholders.

A workshop may be understood as a structured design event in which participants with different backgrounds meet in mutual learning and joining reflection processes where they exchange knowledge and ideas about current or future practice. By engaging people in collaboratively exploring their future, an important part of a workshop is to support mutual learning between different stakeholders in order to facilitate collaborative understanding of current practice and developing vision for the future. Workshops provide venues for this work and they are also events that build relationships across organizations and allow participants to understand each other's perspectives.

Workshop methods come in many variations in relation to the participants, content, and contexts in which the method is applied. Future workshops is one of the most well-established workshop formats in Participatory Design (Kensing and Halskov, 1991) originally developed to help citizen groups have a say in decision-making processes of public planning (Jungk and Müllert, 1987). Variations have been seen over the years, e.g., work with situation cards (Mogensen and Trigg, 1992) and (Ehn and Sjögren, 1991). Among more recent methods is the Inspiration Card Workshop, which combines domain cards and technology cards (Halskov and Dalsgaard, 2006, 2007).

Based on the prior field studies on teenagers' everyday digital practices and on sites of cultural heritage, Case 7, the Digital Natives project (Smith, 2013) initiated a series of workshops in which to explore how the teenagers would reinterpret sites of cultural heritage and visits to the museum (Dindler et al., 2010; Smith, 2013). A series of workshops with teenagers were organized to explore how museums could better support teenagers' motivation for engaging with cultural heritage matters. The workshops were developed from a combination of two well-known workshop methods, Future Workshop (Jungk and Müllert, 1987) and Fictional Inquiry (Dindler and Iversen, 2007), into a dedicated format, designed to enable the teenagers to provide inputs to future digitally supported and engaging exhibition spaces. The workshop series was named "Gaming the Museum" (Dindler et al., 2010), due to the fact that the teenagers used their experience from computer games and leisure time to rethink the exhibition space.

The "Gaming the Museum" workshop took place in an empty exhibition space at a local museum, where a class of 22 teenagers (aged 14–15), their 2 teachers, and 5 researchers participated. The genres of computer games and online communities were chosen, as all teenagers in the previous field studies had expressed motivation for engaging in online activities on a daily basis. The core of the workshop consisted of three parts.

In the first part of the workshop, the teenagers discussed the qualities of one particular game or online community. In the second part, they were asked to create a physical addition or feature to the chosen computer game or online community, using simple props such as paper and cardboard. The physical addition should include the central qualities discussed in the first part. In the final part of the workshop, the teenagers were invited for a 15-minute visit to a current museum exhibition and were given the task to photograph the elements they found interesting. The visit was intended to introduce elements related to cultural heritage into the teenagers' work, but without restricting the teenagers' focus to certain historical narratives. Having visited the museum, the teenagers were assigned the task of creating a new exhibition space for the specific museum, using photos and physical mock-ups made during the second part of the workshop. As an outcome of the Gaming the Museum workshop, the teenagers presented a game-like museum exhibition space for their classmates, teachers, and researchers.

The design method "Gaming the Museum" was derived from two well-known design methods, but adjusted to meet the requirements in this particular design case. The process of designing future exhibition spaces was fun and engaging for the teenagers, and with a point of departure in their own motivation for participating. Analyzing the workshop results provided a good starting point for further concrete codesigning of exhibitions. We will discuss this process in the following section.

Figure 5.3: "Gaming the Museum" workshop. Teenagers reinterpret the museum exhibition space by building a physical installation based on their everyday engagement with computer games.

Case 8, eGov+, working with municipal planners and citizens, similarly deployed a series of workshops based on in-depth interviews with municipal planners and managers, focus group interviews with the two citizen interest groups, as well as two interviews with individual citizens, focusing on the citizens' personal experiences with democratic participation (Bohøj et al., 2011). The focus group interviews used pictures and brainstorming techniques. Workshops were done with municipal planners as well as with citizens to explore the relationship between planning and citizen participation and to motivate the debate further through hands-on exploration of prototypes.

During these activities a broad set of techniques were deployed including future workshops, extreme scenarios, role-playing games, and cultural probes. In narrowing the focus, also scenarios, storyboards, paper prototypes, and mock-ups of various kinds were used. The project constructed role-playing games assigning different roles to citizens asking them to discuss fictive dilemmas, and how such discussions could be supported via mobile technology. Concurrently with the paper prototypes, functional software prototypes for smartphones were developed. With these prototypes the project conducted "walkshops" (Korn and Zander, 2010) urging participants to carry out concrete tasks on the phones, such as the creation of issues on maps, while being out on 30-minute scenario-based walks.

Participatory Design workshops use different means to provide participants with creative or playful means for negotiating the future (Brandt and Grunnet, 2000). Workshops evolving around the use of forum theater methods and magical props have been proposed as a way to create a workshop format for playful collaboration and ideation (Brandt, 2006). In a similar vein, recent contributions have explored various applications of fiction (Iversen and Dindler, 2008; Nägele et al., 2018) and material speculation in participatory practices (Gerber, 2018; Rozendaal et al., 2016). Participatory Design has explored, methodologically in some detail, the inclusion of vulnerable users (Makhaeva et al., 2016; Kanstrup and Bertelsen, 2016; Leong and Iversen, 2015; Lindberg et al., 2014) and children in design. The Interaction Design, and children community in particular, has developed several workshop formats specially targeted at engaging children in Participatory Design workshops (Guha et al., 2004; Walsh et al., 2010; Bekker et al., 2003).

With the background in Future Workshops and with most workshop formats in Participatory Design there is a strong commitment to *democracy* and *empowerment* of participants as well as a focus on *mutual learning* between participants as we have seen in the examples.

## 5.4    COLLABORATIVE PROTOTYPING

Prototyping is a well-known activity in Interaction Design as a way of testing and exploring design ideas. For Participatory Design, prototyping has a distinctly collaborative nature and is best viewed as a process (Floyd, 1984, 1987). Two of the central challenges in collaborative prototyping are to support non-designers in expressing ideas through accessible design materials and allowing for future users to gain hands-on experience with future technology. In Participatory Design, prototypes are, hence, used to establish a design process where both users and designers can participate actively, drawing on their different skills and resources as part of a process of mutual learning (Bødker and Grønbæk, 1991a and 1991b). In order to facilitate collaboration, the prototypes employed should be easy to modify, so that breakdowns caused by bad or incomplete design solutions can rapidly be turned into improved designs by changing the prototype, re-establishing the fluent work-like evaluation of the prototype (Bødker and Grønbæk, 1991a). Modifying the prototype during the prototype session encourages future users to influence the design by stating ideas for improvement (Bødker and Grønbæk, 1991a). This need for easy modifiability of prototypes means that prototyping in Participatory Design involves both simple mock-ups and more advanced software and hardware prototypes as we discuss in Chapter 6.

The idea of cooperative prototyping as a way of establishing understanding, mutual learning, and exploring novel design ideas has been a hallmark of Participatory Design from the outset (Ehn and Kyng, 1991; Bødker and Grønbæk, 1991a). Many different prototyping approaches have been documented: Cederman-Haysom and Brereton (2006) used prototypes to involve dentists in creating ubicomp concepts, Bødker and Grønbæk (1991b) developed innovative hypertext concepts together with urban planners, and Hertzum and Simonsen (2010) demonstrated how the long-term deployment of prototypes in work contexts lead to deeper understanding among participants. Also, studies in Participatory Design have addressed the challenges of remote prototyping involving people who are not physically co-located (Hargreaves and Robertson, 2012) or e-prototyping (Bleek et al., 2002).

As preparation for prototyping, the working group must establish a common understanding of the aims of the process, the status of the intermediate products developed in the process, and the role of prototyping in the overall design process. Ideally, cooperative prototyping sessions should be performed by a small group of designers and users with access to flexible computer-based tools for the rapid development and modification of prototypes (Bødker and Grønbæk, 1991a). It is important that the working group is established together with skilled user representatives. With respect to context, the cooperative prototyping, the session must take place in a simulated future work situation or, even better, in a real use situation. The product of the prototyping process is more than a computer prototype. Cooperative prototyping aims at being a learning process rather than an evaluation, aiming both at exploring design options and spreading new understandings to workers and managers who are not participating directly in the prototyping session. To plan a prototyping session, the designers must consider the purpose of the prototyping session, how stable the prototype should be in advance, to what extent in-session modifications should be possible, which settings to host the setting in, and how to evaluate and document the outcome of the cooperative prototyping session. In this way designers create conditions for participants to influence the design decisions during the prototyping session (Bødker and Grønbæk, 1991a).

It is important to notice that prototypes have a role to play beyond giving users the means for hands-on experience and trying out their practices against a future technology. Prototypes have also been used in Participatory Design to "provoke" and point to alternatives that are not directly deployable in use. Mogensen (1992) talks about "provotyping" to address this, and Kannabiran and Bødker (2020) discuss prototypes as ways of capturing and exploring the not yet known, in continuation also of Bødker and Christiansen's (2004) search for means in Participatory Design to capture new forms of activities that are in the making, rather than Participatory Design for replacing tools in existing practices.

Based on field studies and workshops with teenagers, programers, and researchers, the Digital Natives project, Case 7, moved toward collaborative prototyping sessions in which the participants jointly developed ideas for new engagements with materials on cultural heritage. Many of the teenagers were very engaged in electronic music production and wanted music and music creation to be an integral part of the exhibition. During the sessions, they demonstrated how their activity around music production emerged from their own lifeworlds and by interacting with friends around the world. Some of the programers had previously been engaged in an interactive exhibition in a rock-museum and brought ideas from this project to the table. Finding synergies between the teenagers and the programers, the group jointly explored how the music-making practices of teenagers and the interactive installation could embrace some of the initial ideas for a museum exhibition that was developed in the initial phase of the project. The idea of a "DJ Station" in which participants could collaboratively and creatively engage in music-making around an interactive table emerged through multiple iterations of drawings, cardboard mock-ups, and horizontal prototypes before it was brought to life. The final "DJ Station" became an interactive and audiovisual installation based on a tangible user interface with fiducial tracking (unique tags that enable the system to recognize specific music loops). The DJ Station allowed the audience to interact with the musical universe of the seven digital natives involved in the project, while getting first-hand experience with the remix and mash-up cultures that are hallmarks of the digital natives' generation (Smith and Iversen, 2011). Each young native was represented in the installation by a cube (with visible fiduciary markers), which played musical loops when placed on the table surface.

Figure 5.4: Collaborative prototyping session in which teenagers, designers, and programers developed new concepts and prototypes for engaging museum exhibitions.

Figure 5.5: Collaborative prototyping sessions with teenagers, designers and programrs lead to the development of an interactive table in which teenagers could bring music samples and collaboratively create new music.

Similarly in Case 8, eGov+, all of the activities described above contributed to an iterative design process where prototypes were developed and used as alternative suggestions that provided potential users with the possibility of exploring the issue hands-on. Moreover, the prototypes served as a way of probing the context of citizen participation in municipal planning (see more in Chapter 7).

Collaborative prototyping gives specific means and ways of helping users understand design proposals and *future* practices, also in the specific as hands-on experience. Sometimes collaborative prototyping also raises questions and helps understand current skills and practices, and in both capacities, collaborative prototyping is change-oriented and supports *empowerment* and emancipation regarding both individuals and communities/organizational units.

Figure 5.6: Audiences engage with the DJ Station in the Digital Natives exhibition.

## 5.5    INFRASTRUCTURING

By infrastructuring we refer to the activities in which designers and users as participants collabo-ratively establish social, organizationa, and technical infrastructures in order to ascertain that the results of the project can be sustained after the project ends. Among the core issues for Participatory Design has been a concern for ensuring that participants and future users actually enjoy lasting results and gains from a Participatory Design effort. Bødker (1996) argues that it is important to put the organization in a position where experiences can be used beyond the project. Long-term gains and results may take on many forms such as products, skills, or increased democratic influence. Also, sustainability of project achievements may range from merely maintaining what has been accomplished to more ambitious aims of scaling up achievements (Iversen and Dindler, 2014). We address the issue of sustainability in more detail in Chapter 10. The notion of infrastructuring has surfaced relatively recently in the Participatory Design literature although the idea is older (Star and Ruhleder, 1994). As such, the term is still used in a variety of ways related to Participatory Design (see Karasti, 2014 for discussion) and we use the term in a broad sense to cover the various social, technical, and organizational constellations that are created to ensure that a project's achievement may be sustained or developed beyond the project.

The early work within Participatory Design identified the need for "continuing design in use" by creating platforms that could be tailored and adapted over time. This concern has roots in Nygaard's vision of domain-specific or profession-oriented programming languages and environments (Kaasbøll, 1983). It is also echoed in Fischer and Lembke's (1987) work with tailoring environments as well as in the research of Mørch (1997) and Pipek and Kahler (2006). Mørch et al. (2004) framed the area now known as end-user development and programming. These works share a concern for open and adaptable technical platforms. The means needed for users to contribute in such settings have remained a focus for Participatory Design. Kaptelinin and Bannon (2012) have more recently discussed design processes as a duality of intrinsic and extrinsic practice transformation and point to the differences between these two processes also in terms of tools needed by the users for their intrinsic development vs. the tools needed for development that comes from outside.

Beyond the need for adaptable technical systems, authors have also explored the significance of social infrastructures in terms of sustainability. In their work, Carroll and Rosson (2007) demonstrate the importance of strong social networks within communities and Dindler and Iversen (2014) discuss the need for a "relational expertise" among Participatory Design practitioners. In terms of the organizational efforts needed to create infrastructures for sustaining project achievements, Participatory Design emerged from an explicit political agenda of user empowerment and democratization (Bjerknes et al., 1987). As such, organizational structures to support these political ambitions have pervaded parts of the Participatory Design literature. Among the most recent contributions to this strand of work is Kyng's (2015) discussion of the challenge of maintaining democratic control of the results of the Participatory Design processes.

It is hard to identify specific methods that have infrastructuring as their sole purpose. Rather, it may be argued that concerns for infrastructuring may be more or less articulated within the established methods presented above. For example, workshops and cooperative prototyping may address the organizational structures that will support or address technical infrastructures. Dindler and Iversen (2014) make the case that much of the work going on within and between workshops and meetings is relational work in which participants build and consolidate the networks and relationships that will support the project beyond its completion. Arguably the best example of successful infrastructuring Participatory Design practice is the work in the Living Lab at Malmö,[2] where a design approach has been developed, based on community engagement promoting democratic dialogue (see Ehn et al., 2014). The aim is for users to influence how to improve quality of life in a real life context. Rather than considering design as a clearly delineated "project," the Living lab approach promotes long-term engagement, building trust, and establishing venues for democratic dialogues about the future. The work in the Malmö Living Lab initiative very literally embodies the

---

[2] http://medea.mah.se/malmo-living-labs/.

core Participatory Design ideas of politics and context and challenges in the pursuit of designing alternatives in collaboration with communities.

Infrastructuring is closely connected to ongoing ways of connecting future practices and current skills and resources. *Empowerment* of people is hence connected to participation in these longer-term processes.

## 5.6    EVALUATION

By evaluation we refer to the activities in which future users and stakeholders assess the qualities of a design product and the outcomes emerging from the design process. For Participatory Design, outcomes may be tangible in the form of products and more intangible in the form of visions of future technologies, a new organizational structure, new skills developed, or knowledge acquired.

Participatory Design researchers conduct mostly informal evaluations during and after their project. These evaluations are hard to engage with from the outside as they are rarely reported in a detailed manner. Among the papers that do assess the outcomes of Participatory Design projects, there is a general tendency to use qualitative methods and to define the criteria of evaluation only after the project. We have devoted much of Chapter 9 for a thorough discussion of evaluation practices in Participatory Design projects.

Here we focus mainly on examples of how to do such evaluations. Early work by Kensing et al. (1996) suggests concrete methods for evaluating Participatory Design projects highlighting the importance of evaluation of both process and products within organizational contexts. Merkel et al. (2004) stress the importance of also accounting for indirect and long-term changes within communities when evaluating Participatory Design. The approach taken by Frauenberger et al. (2015), as discussed in Chapter 5, focuses on rigor and accountability, where accountability is understood in terms of linking collaborative work with decisions and outcomes in a transparent way and rigor is understood as internal validity in the process.

In relation to the Digital Natives project, Case 7, and other similar projects within cultural heritage communication, a certain way of accounting for the participants' gains from participating has been used (Bossen et al., 2010). The techniques are centered around interview studies 1–3 years after the project ends. The timing of the evaluation studies are controversial in the sense that this happens after the project has ended and the funding has run out. However, this is the best way to account for the impact of a project and to analyze how it has changed the life or the practices of our collaborators. The interview is concerned with matters related to the participants:

- influence on the project and product;

- most satisfying and most frustrating experiences;

- personal gain from participation;

- new quality of work, new possibilities discovered, or more influence on own work conditions;

- new areas of competence acquired;

- subsequent shifts in career or choice of education, owing to the project;

- extent of new outlook on technology or personal practices;

- overall assessment of participation in the project; and

- newly emerged opportunities in general.

These questions are examples of how the strong commitment of Participatory Design are reflected in evaluation and help shed light on which questions to ask, and then at least indirectly to which results to aim for in the design processes, in contrast to, e.g., the usability measures and more known from standard HCI textbooks. Such forms of evaluation may still be useful, but we caution that they should not dominate the evaluation.

## 5.7    SUMMARY

In this chapter we have seen how Participatory Design can be characterized in terms of the main activities that practitioners engage in: field studies, workshops, collaborative prototyping, infrastructuring and evaluation. Participatory Design shares methods and tools with many other design disciplines, but Participatory Design is distinct in terms of the way in which methods are deployed. In targeting commitments such as future practices and emancipation, it is quite evident that Participatory Design takes a wider approach than standard Interaction Design models and that, e.g., the idea of establishing requirements and matching future alternatives with requirements is more difficult. Participatory Design also looks further ahead and combines existing technologies and structures with future technologies through infrastructuring, a supplementary way of dealing with human practices as changing. With the focus on democracy and learning in particular, designers and researchers may be less directly deciding on next steps in the design processes. This is true however, at the same time as the researchers/designers are the ones who bring their professional PD skills to the table. We shall look further at tools and materials for Participatory Design in Chapter 6.

### Read More

Materializing Participatory Design's ambitions and ideals in specific tools and techniques has received considerable attention through the years. Attempts have been made to provide overviews of what can be considered Participatory Design-specific methods and taxonomies to describe their qualities (Muller and Kuhn, 1993; Sanders et al., 2010). Early overviews were practice-based reporting from a nascent research community (Greenbaum and Kyng, 1991; Schuler and Namioka, 1993) connecting methods, cases and emerging theoretical understandings. Other overviews, such as Munk-Madsen and Kensing (1993), have sought to structure and organize methods and tools according to the kind of knowledge they produce by distinguishing between abstract knowledge and concrete experience on the one hand, and between users' present work, technological options, and the new system on the other. Overviews have also been provided from within HCI where Muller and Druin (2012) characterized Participatory Design practices that create "hybridity" and establish a "third space" of HCI. The latest contribution to the overviews of Participatory Design methods is found in Simonsen and Robertson (2012), who dedicated two chapters to methods, tools, and techniques. The bi-annual PDC conference and the journal of *Co-Design* are currently among the most prominent venues reporting on novel Participatory Design methods and their application.

CHAPTER 6

# What Are the Tools and Materials of Participatory Design?

This chapter looks into the tools and materials of Participatory Design. Participatory Design makes use of a number of tools and materials that aid both the collaboration in the joint activities, the documentation of design suggestions and the hands-on activities that pervade Participatory Design. Many of these tools and materials are not unique to Participatory Design but the way in which they are used is fundamentally shaped by the kinds of activities that PD practitioners undertake. In this chapter we highlight four central aspects of the way tools and materials are used in Participatory Design as:

1. tools for communicating and creating exchanges between stakeholders with different backgrounds;

2. easily accessible design materials that invite non-experts to take on an active hands-on role in design activities;

3. props that are used to scaffold and support workshops activities; and

4. manifestations that point to the future.

With a starting point in Cases 7 and 8, in particular, you will learn about the tools and see detailed examples. In particular, you will see how the tools of Participatory Design are important because they provide recognizability, transparency, and understandability in the design process, combined with hands-on experience for *users*. You will also learn about how prototypes and other tools support the work of *designers*, and that really successful tools create a bridge between these merits for the two groups, in the "third space" *between them*, hence you will learn how tools support the four strong commitments: democracy and empowerment, in terms of transparency, understandability, and hands-on experience; and mutual learning between designers and users in development of users' future practices through tools that hold onto future solutions, in particular prototypes.

## 6.1 MOCK-UPS

Mock-ups are made with paper and everyday materials and often used in early parts of cooperative prototyping. Mundane and tangible materials such as paper and cardboard were widely used in the early Participatory Design projects, and hailed for their ability to facilitate participation from people without any technical expertise. Ehn and Kyng (1991) made the case that the low-fidelity mock-ups of Participatory Design made sense because they allowed the creation of "shared language games" in which both designers and users could take part.

The most important elements of mock-ups use everyday materials recognizable by the users and present possibilities of (primitive) hands-on exploration by the users, be this regarding the direct interaction with the future technology or, e.g., collaboration between several users around the technology. The Utopia project, Case 2, used cardboard boxes to indicate the position of printers and to discuss the role of printing in collaboration between typographers and journalists. It also used paper mock-ups and back-projected pictures to illustrate high-resolution full-page editing on screen (Figure 6.1). The mock-ups of Utopia also included design of hardware, specifically pointing devices suited for typography (Figure 6.2). It was largely in the Utopia project that the notion of mock-ups as means for users to do hands-on exploration was invented.

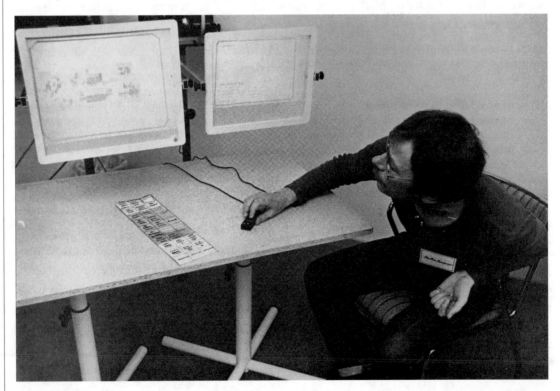

Figure 6.1: Back-screen projection mock-up from the Utopia project. ©Greenbaum and Kyng (1991).

Figure 6.2: Design/mock-up of four different pointing devices from Utopia. ©Greenbaum and Kyng (1991).

In Case 7, Digital Natives, paper and cardboard mock-ups were used by children in the museum to do their own initial design, as discussed also in Chapter 5. In Case 8, eGov+, the project made use of paper prototypes as early and easily changeable versions of a mobile app for location-based discussions of planning issues, based on initial interviews. Paper prototypes were developed over several iterations with users, before turning to more advanced prototyping tools (see Section 6.2).

Paper, sticky notes, and cardboard have been used for mocking up in many different kinds of settings, where users have been actively involved, e.g., second screens in flexible offices (Bødker and Christiansen, 2004), family homes (Hutchinson et al., 2003), remote schools (Bødker and Sundblad, 2007), and many other settings.

Mock-ups serve as easily accessible design materials that invite non-experts to take on an active hands-on role in design activities. They help manifest design ideas and possible solutions. Hence, they also are tools for communication between stakeholders with different backgrounds where they scaffold and support workshops activities.

## 6.2    PROTOTYPING TOOLS

Bødker and Grønbæk (1991a and 1991b) used what was known as Hypercard to prototype, in sessions with users present or in small iterations. Hypercard was deployed on early Macs and combined a database, a graphical, flexible, modifiable interfac, and built-in programming language that made rapid, explorative development possible. Further explorations of Hypercard prototypes were carried out by Grønbæk and Mogensen (1997) regarding document management in a large inspection organization.

Exploratory prototypes were introduced into Participatory Design by the Utopia project, Case 2, even though at that time, there were few prototyping tools available. Historically, prototypes have been used in cases with children in both schools and less formal educational settings (museums) by Benford et al. (2000) as well as Dindler et al. (2005).

Several projects at Aarhus University in the 1980–90s introduced, into Participatory Design, prototyping processes where prototypes would be solid enough to be tried out in a real-life setting over periods of weeks (with support). In the AT project, extensive effort was put into developing early versions of mobile prototypes to be used by labor inspectors who spent extensive time on the roads (Bødker, 1993). EuroCOOP/EuroCODE was a big European Union funded project that worked with construction inspection on a major building site, that of the Great Belt Bridge, which was at the time the longest suspension bridge in the world. As part of this project, two prototypes were developed that were deployed at the offices of the inspection officers: One that combined computing with paper and other things to explore the possibilities of augmented paper, and one that focused more specifically on documentation to be used for future repair (Bouvin et al., 1996; Mackay et al., 1995; Grønbæk and Mogensen, 1997; Grønbæk et al., 1993; Mogensen, 1992). With many newer forms of computing, such as the Internet of Things, such mixed forms of prototyping materials have become more prominent.

Case 8, eGov+, that worked with urban local planning among citizens and planners, worked extensively with prototypes combining mobile applications for Android and a web-based prototype for the desktop (Bohøj et al., 2011). These prototypes provided two ways of viewing the same information based on what is best suited for the mobile discussion and planning situation.

The outset for discussions was a geographically located topic as the collection point for information such as descriptions, comments and pictures. For screenshots of the mobile prototype, see Figure 6.3. This first web-based software prototype was used to gain feedback from planners. However, more functionality, such as adding pictures from the built-in camera, were needed and hence the process was supplemented with a mobile app. This mobile prototype was developed in several steps from paper prototypes. It showed topics on a map and allowed for commenting on these topics.

Figure 6.3: Screenshots from the mobile eGov+ prototype: (a) the map view, (b) the list of topics, (c) creating a new topic, and (d) viewing a topic. ©Bohøj et al. (2011).

The project developed a mobile and a desktop prototype to emphasize the different ways information could be presented. The larger screen area available on the desktop made it possible to present more information at the same time and not having to switch back and forth between views as on the mobile phone. The planners explored prototypes in a future workshop, leading to a proposal to work with 3D-models for contemplation at site "through" the smartphone. The workshop participants found this idea intriguing, but wanted to know more. The planners also wanted to be able to see the level of activity among citizens so that they could quickly see where discussions were heading. This led to a further focus on the visualization of activity.

Figure 6.4: Trying out a mobile prototype in eGov+. ©Bohøj et al. (2011).

Case 8, eGov+, is an example of how different prototypes were combined and activated in the Participatory Design process. However, the case also illustrates that there were no good prototyping tools available and the designers hence had to work directly with, for example, the platform of Android phones.

It may be somewhat surprising that platforms similar to Hypercard have been hard to find in the many years to follow, even though rapid prototyping tools for specific platforms and domains do exist. Hence, such open, dynamic platforms are still a concern for research (see, e.g., Tchernavskij et al., 2017) and the Webstrates/Codestartes family of tools (Borowski et al., 2018) is one example of tools that may eventually fill this space.

Prototypes, compared to mock-ups, help exploration of dynamic aspects of use. They may be less easily accessible for all as design materials at the same time as they give better support for active hands-on experience. They manifest the future in ways that give more detailed support for the further work of designers. Indeed the sophistication of prototyping tools vary and may be more needed for some types of prototyping than others.

## 6.3    DATA

Traditionally, data has been a challenge for Participatory Design because it has been difficult to populate prototypes with relevant data to make prototypes recognizable to users (Bødker and Grønbæk, 1991b). Data has, however, increasingly become a material for many organizations both internally and also when it comes to public and municipal organizations, in the interaction between the public organization and the citizens. Activating users at large to participate in design with data, and in particular also to engage citizens, has hence become an issue for Participatory Design. Lotado and DiSalvo (2018) used the format of hackathons to address data as material in civic settings.

Data, as material for engaging citizens with their environment, has also been the focus for toolkits such as citizen sensing toolkits (Balestrini et al., 2015).[3] Participatory sensing, as this is called (Coulsen et al., 2018), is a bottom-up approach to data collection led by citizens and with some form of problem or commitment to their community.

Data used in Participatory Design mainly provides tools for communicating and creating exchanges between stakeholders with different backgrounds. They are used as props to scaffold and support workshops activities, mainly by providing background in support of the interests of certain users or user communities.

## 6.4    DIAGRAMS AND DESCRIPTIONS

Since many software development and engineering methods are dependent on specifications such as UML diagrams, it is not uncommon that users are asked to participate in or provide, e.g., job flow description. This phenomenon is not new. As a matter of fact, this kind of specification exercises have existed since the 1970s and what was called systems description with users is an early phenomenon in Participatory Design, dating back to the NJMF, Case 1, and its sister projects (Kaasbø, 1983). It was well known that while participating in making such descriptions was, to some extent, useful for participating users, the diagrams as such were not helpful beyond that. This was what set the Utopia project, Case 2, on the track to hands-on prototyping, the problem being that users generally struggle not only with the specification methods, but also with explicating their own, often tacit, knowledge of their work.

Hence, UML diagrams and other (formal) specifications may help designers and programmers for whom they create manifestations of future technology. At the same time they have limited utility in Participatory Design, and generally in the interaction between designers and future users.

---

[3] https://docs.smartcitizen.me/.

## 6.5   STICKY NOTES AND PICTURES

All of the above are examples of tools that also include material that in some form or other point toward a future running technology. This is indeed not always the case and, e.g., sticky notes have for many years been the conventional tool for sorting exercises, affinity diagramming and brainstorming both within groups of designers and between designers and users. Christensen et al. (2020) outline the history of sticky notes, in particular with focus on creativity and design processes. Used in Participatory Design, sticky notes are versatile in the ways they are for design at large, and they share with cardboard boxes that they handle easily and are recognizable because of their everyday nature, by users.

Pictures to serve as inspiration and also point to specific use activities or situations have been used in many kinds of Participatory Design workshops. Video cards and experience clips (Isomursu et al., 2004), as well as a number of other types of pictures, are used for various forms of workshops (Buur and Søndergaard 2000, Tschudy et al., 1996).

Case 8, eGov+, used sticky notes together with future workshops, and with citizens, also combined with various role-playing games. A deck of pictures (Figure 6.5) of our built world and nature was used in combination with these early activities to help both planners and citizens focus on challenges regarding local planning. The pictures were deliberately chosen to not focus on any particular topic or issue. Case 7, Digital Natives, contains many examples of the use of pictures in the processes of doing design with teenagers.

Figure 6.5: Picture game with citizens in eGov+.

Sticky notes and pictures mainly serve as easily accessible design materials that invite non-experts to take on an active hands-on role in design activities. They are props that are used to scaffold and support workshops activities by their versatility.

## 6.6    PROBES AND SPECULATIVE MATERIALS

A recent development within Participatory Design is the use of speculation and fiction as parts of workshops and collaborative explorations. Rozendaal et al. (2016) propose a workshop in which researchers engage with embodied speculation, and explore how it can become a tool to help users and researchers engage in dialogue about the social opportunities and ethical implications of emerging technologies. Knutz et al. (2016) explore how fiction can be a resource for Participatory Design to evoke various forms of participation. They present several examples of participatory prototyping, which use play or games to engage participants with a particular use of make-believe using, e.g., Hussain and Sanders' (2012) paper-doll toolkit. Gerber (2018) used speculation to create Speculative props (theatrical props) that are "designed to materialize community members' visions to provoke conversation around our utopias and their negative implications." These speculations are intended to confront challenges around public participation, collaborative visioning, and the long process of enacting radical systemic change.

Speculation as design fiction has also played its part in Nägele et al.'s (2018) work on Participatory Design fiction. Using data gathered in probes, Nägele et al. (2018) use a workshop to co-create design fictions that are meant to give voice to the participants.

Speculation and fiction are increasingly used in Participatory Design research, however as the examples show, it is often done using craft material (as in Hussain and Sanders' (2012) paper-dolls or Nägele et al.'s (2018) sketched design fictions) or mundane everyday artifacts [as seen in Dindler et al. (2005) and Iversen and Dindler (2008)].

The Digital Natives and eGov+ projects, Cases 7 and 8, both used fiction and role playing as part of the Participatory Design processes. Their materials and tools mostly consisted of familiar everyday objects. In both instances, one could imagine exploring more radical alternatives, utilizing more elaborate probes and materials.

Material probes were introduced in order to solicit speculative feedback from users as they are in their own setting (Gaver et al., 1999; Mattelmäki, 2008). Probes were consisting of packages of, e.g., postcards and cameras that made it easy to send feedback back to designers and were introduced as a means of provoking inspirational responses from a group of users (Gaver et al., 1999) and more recently discussed also with respect to how probes offer different modes of inquiry in co-exploring activities (Knutz et al., 2016). Probes have, in HCI at large, also been extended from these speculative approaches to generally soliciting information from users in their own settings. This we will not discuss any further. Also, probes do not, as such, lead to Participatory Design. However, both the gathering of feedback and the use of the submitted pictures, postcards, etc. can indeed be used in Participatory Design activities in similar ways as, e.g., pictures (Section 6.5) namely as easily accessible design materials for non-experts and props that are used to scaffold and support workshops activities.

## 6.7  SUMMARY

The list of tools and suggestions for tools for Participatory Design is long, and has inspiration from other design fields. It has been important for our selection here that the tools have a focus on information technologies or that they are frequently used in this context and in Participatory Design. Also, the cases we discuss have made choices and used some tools and not others, sometimes to match the core activities presented in Figure 5.1 and other times for less well-described reasons.

We have exemplified in this chapter tools for communicating and creating exchanges between stakeholders with different backgrounds, easily accessible design materials that invite non-experts to take on an active hands-on role in design activities, props that are used to scaffold and support workshops activities, and manifestations that point to the future. Some of the mentioned tools and materials serve some of these purposes better than others and we have also given examples of well-known design materials and tools that are frequent but do not serve the core of Participatory Design terribly well because they don't bridge well between the understandability of users and the needs to designers to manifest and hold on to design decisions. Hence, there is no straightforward choice of a set of tools and materials that up front will support the strong commitments of Participatory Design.

### Read More

Brodersen Hansen (2017) gives a good overview of tools and materials of design more generally and Participatory Design in particular. Munk-Madsen and Kensing (1993) present an early discussion of the PD toolbox.

# CHAPTER 7

# How Is Participatory Design Organized?

In the previous chapters we have addressed activities, methods, tools, and materials used in Participatory Design. As we have of course also mentioned, it is an important principle of Participatory Design to organize design and development so as to involve users in various ways. This is partly done through the tools and techniques mentioned in the previous chapters, but as with any process Participatory Design requires organization. Participatory Design is not, however, about direct collaboration between researchers/designers and users all the time, as we also saw in Chapter 6. Organizing Participatory Design projects also means handling a division of work in the project, and with our concerns here, specifically a division of work between professional designers and researchers on the one hand and the users on the other. Hence, the organization of Participatory Design processes also includes concerns for which users, stakeholders, or groups are active and when.

With this chapter you will learn more about the principles to organize Participatory Design processes. The chapter focuses on four important principles for Participatory Design:

1. mutual learning as central to the organization of Participatory Design;

2. iteration for the organization of Participatory Design processes;

3. tying activities involving users and stakeholders in relevant ways into a process; and

4. vertical processes of decision making in Participatory Design.

We focus on organizing and the division of work between groups involved in Participatory Design projects. This organization plays out at various scales and in various dimensions. The dimensions include the organization of work internally between professional researchers, designers, and developers; the organization of and division of work between various groups of users and stakeholders; and most importantly, the organization of and division of work between users on the one hand and researchers/designers on the other. The scales that we look at include division of work over the duration of the process, horizontally across groups of users and stakeholders, and vertically at different levels of organizational and political decision-making.

With division of work also follows the means and activities that hold together the process as a whole and those that connect the activities, often behind the scene, or *backstage* as Bødker et al. (2017) discuss, in contrast to clear and well-defined workshops with users that are on the *frontstage* and often showcased in research papers (see Chapters 6 and 7).

Participatory Design projects, like we discuss here, are examples of collaborative activities where designers and users collaborate over time, with people coming and leaving the activities. Schmidt and Bannon (1992) talk about articulation work as the activities that it takes to divide, allocate, coordinate, schedule, mesh, interrelate, etc. collaborative activities. Principles for organizing the Participatory Design processes include the means to plan, coordinate etc. the activities that make Participatory Design processes progress, while making the most out of the involvement of users as well as of the contributions of researchers, designers, and other stakeholders.

The main takeaway is that Participatory Design is iterative and focused on mutual learning. Participatory Design does not mean equal participation of users and designers at all stages in the process. Dividing work in the best manners may help plan the design process and bring in the appropriate Participatory Design methods at appropriate times. This also means that Participatory Design activities need to take place at many vertical levels of decision-making which also then involve people as users though they are not and will never be direct users of the technology in question.

The following will look at some more examples of how this is done.

## 7.1    MUTUAL LEARNING AND ORGANIZING PROCESSES

The core principle of mutual learning is essential to how Participatory Design divides work and extends over time (Bødker et al., 2017). Mutual learning is framed as a way of finding common ground among participating designers and users, and ways of working in the process (Kensing and Greenbaum, 2013), to build trust among participants (Bratteteig et al., 2013) and to share power within the project (Bratteteig and Wagner, 2016). As pointed out by Bødker and Christiansen (2004), only when a design team has fundamental knowledge of existing practices will it be possible to arrive at a sustained design.

Mutual learning has been the driving force in PD projects since the early years. The Utopia project, Case 2, developed their catalog of tools, in particular workshops and prototyping/mock-ups (Chapter 7) with a concern specifically for mutual learning (Ehn and Kyng, 1984). In specific, mutual learning is planned and initiated by the researchers/designers based on a concern about what they get out of engaging with users [a concern they share with, e.g., Contextual Design, (Holtzblatt and Beyer, 1997; Beyer, 2010)]. The additional concern regarding mutual learning, is, however, also to understand, plan for, and convey what users get out of the mutual activities, often specifically what the users may learn, and how they may be empowered to act.

Pape and Thoresen's (1987) notion of empowerment is used by Bødker (1996) to suggest that Participatory Design work is not only about work and achievements within a project, but also about putting the organization in a position where experiences may be used after the project ends. A similar idea is found in the MUST method (Kensing et al., 1996), where sustainability is a grounding principle in ensuring that new technical systems fit preferred work practices and in Carroll et al.'s

(2000) discussion of their long-term project. The STEPS (Software Technology for Evolutionary Participatory Systems development) model was developed by Floyd and her colleagues to emphasize iterative processes and mutual learning (Floyd et al., 1989). Grønbæk et al. (1993) used their Participatory Design work in a large EU-funded project with construction inspectors and their documentation to propose CESD (Cooperative Experimental System Development) that in particular makes it possible to plan and reflect on activities, methods, and activities, separately and together over time.

## 7.2    ITERATION

STEPS and CESD are examples of Participatory Design processes that emphasize iteration. Iteration has been a concern in systems and software development since the models early on were breaking with the waterfall model and other similar linear process models (Royce, 1987). For Participatory Design, iteration has the additional importance that users can better relate to and understand prototypes (see Chapters 5 and 6) than they can traditional requirement specifications.

Just like most modern models of Interaction Design and user-centered design are iterative, and even formulated as an ISO standard,[4] this is true also for Participatory Design, which is less focused on one final system than the ISO model. However, the activities that we present in this book generally happen in iteration and going back and forth between analyzing and understanding user practice, constructing, e.g., prototypes, and evaluating them with users in various forms.

A founding father of agile development, Cockburn, hailed Participatory Design as an important source of inspiration for agile development (Cockburn, 2001). Participatory methods and related user centered methods have also been explored for agile development processes which are otherwise mainly iterative for the purpose of iteration among developers, with little concern for the users. Beyer (2010), e.g., discusses Contextual Design integrated with agile development, and Begnum and Thorkildsen (2015) compare the methods deployed by comparing user-centered methods in agile and non-agile processes. Kautz (2010) presents a specific real-life case of a German, agile design project and analyzes user participation in the methods used and the roles of users and designers in the process.

Seen as an overall principle of organization for PD processes, iteration allows us to divide the process in parts that involve both users and developers/designers in appropriate chunks that can be assessed along the way. Where users are mainly involved through some of the activities, through techniques and tools discussed in Chapters 6 and 7, this does not mean that users and developers take equal part in all activities. Preece et al.'s (2019) interaction design model iterates between analyses of existing practices to establish requirements, designing to suggest alternatives to meet these requirements, prototyping to build and make ideas available to users, and finally evaluating to

---

[4]  https://www.iso.org/obp/ui/#iso:std:iso:9241:-210:ed-2:v1:en.

ensure the quality of the design. The model (Figure 5.1) in Chapter 5 emphasizes mutual learning, as discussed above, and iteration both among the activities and through the active use of prototyping and infrastructuring. Bødker et al. (2017) talk about these well-defined activities where users are involved as frontstage, and contrast those with the messier backstage activities where designers, developers, and other groups of professionals do activities to manage the processes, and to actually, e.g., build the prototypes that users are presented with. In a way, the backstage activities are implicit in most models, including the two mentioned, and we will discuss this phenomenon further below.

## 7.3    DIVIDING THE WORK, BACKSTAGE

With such methods as presented in Section 7.2 as with Participatory Design in general, it does not mean that users participate equally in all activities in the process, and even more, what it means to participate may vary a lot at different stages and activities in the process. Hence, not all activities are with all users in Participatory Design, and not all involved users are necessarily direct future users of the technological solutions for a process to qualify as Participatory Design.

Kyng (1995) outlines a simple model describing different activities/methods and to what extent they involve users and designers/developers. We have simplified the model a little in Figure 7.1. Therefore, the activities include frontstage, well-defined activities where users are involved as well as backstage activities that are at times less well designed in scope and extend in particular when it comes to, e.g., technological implementation. Kyng's model does not include the work that it takes to manage and keep the process going, and this work we'll return to.

In a somewhat orthogonal view of the design process, Obendorf et al. (2009) make a distinction between activities where specific future users and developers focus on specific tasks and features (such as when, e.g., a developer interviews a user, when they explore a prototype together), activities that address the organization, and practices where users and developers both may participate through some form of representation and where methods may include field studies and workshops. And finally, activities bridge several user organizations where users represent particular interests and where visions and values are in focus. This level of community of interest is that Obendorf et al. (2009) talk about when they discuss how to organize intercontextual design processes: Deliberate design attempts to make users and designers meet across specific project and organizational boundaries so as to develop the bigger infrastructuring project and support learning across projects and units. Bødker et al. (2017) call this *horizontal reach* and address the ability of a project to connect among similar communities of practice. For example, teachers (in Case 6) in one school connect to groups of teachers at another school. This model is an example of ways of planning, organizing, and managing the design process, more than the actual activities involving the users. Agile models and similar also contain specific ways of planning and estimating the activities, and, e.g., Beyer (2010) presents an estimation process for implementation of user stories. Such backstage processes borrow tools and techniques from many types of methods.

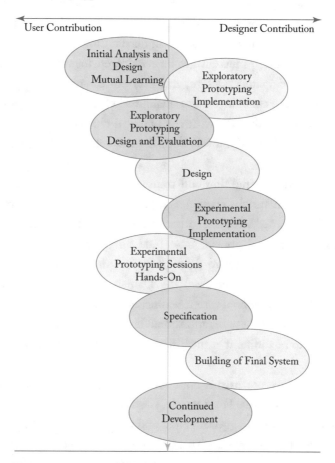

Figure 7.1: Kyng's (1995) model for balancing user and designer activities in Participatory Design. Simplified redrawing. In this figure we identify the frontstage activities (left side) and the backstage (right side), while illustrating that frontstage/backstage is more of a spectrum than an absolute.

Common to these models and processes are that they not only deal iteratively with the specific design process and the specific users. They also focus on sustaining the processes and experiences beyond the specific design process, and they work with technical and organizational infrastructuring through processes that continuously look at what is there, in terms of technological and organizational means, skills, decision processes, etc. and what the potentials are for change of these same means.

## 7.4    VERTICAL ORGANIZATION OF PROCESSES

Ehn (1989) had a very principled discussion of how Participatory Design is a way of handling the dialectical relationship of tradition and transcendence regarding the classical theoretical foundations of research and design. Using the Marxist understanding of dialectics, he argued that the traditions of research and design must always be considered together with the interdisciplinary practical challenges of Participatory Design, and they are always also opposite of one another. This confrontation will in the concrete lead to qualitative change. He argued that by confronting classical theoretical schools of thought with the practical challenges of working with users and their needs, it is, hence, possible to innovate both the theoretical traditions and the technologies to be used by users.

Bringing the concern for tradition and transcendence to life in real-life projects talks to the division of work between various competencies in the project and how traditions need to be brought together and confronted with each other to bring change/transcendence.

Using the FabLab@School project, Case 6, as an example, Bødker et al. (2017) discuss Participatory Design activities set up to fully grasp, and design with, the complex and highly decentralized infrastructure of (in this case) the Danish educational system. First of all, they point out that for the FabLab@School case it was necessary to include and consider stakeholders, participants, and activities at all these organizational levels. Second the participants and activities, hence methods, needed to be different at the different levels, and hence participation is essentially different between levels.

Several of the cases we use in this book have similar, but often less complicated, vertical structures of interests and concerns. For example, Case 8 carried out a process where specific designs were carried out with specific governmental and citizen users in specific design projects. At the same time, the project collaborated with users and management of three municipalities, and with companies supplying technologies for municipalities through an ongoing series of workshops where materials and designs from the specific design projects were activated and discussed (see, e.g., Bødker and Zander, 2015). Bødker and Zander (2015) discuss the challenges of municipal democracy which are characterized by increasing professionalization and expert rule when it comes to municipal decision making, as at the same time fewer citizens are members of political parties and public support for local politicians is dwindling. At the same time, cause-based engagement is increasing. Bødker and Zander (2015) conclude that *"this may mean that citizens are dissatisfied with the current concrete form of municipality decision-making, but remain loyal to its abstract idea and open to new forms of participation."* Hence, the process of decision making when it comes to Participatory Design projects with both citizens and municipal workers of various kinds is one place where the vertical involvement is important and possibly needs to take new forms.

Bødker et al. (2017) list the core Participatory Design activities for Case 5, in relation to the levels of authority to which they were directed (see Figure 7.2). Compared to the majority of Participatory Design research projects, this activity list diverges in several ways. They point out that some of the core activities in Figure 6.4 would often be considered as outside the scope of Participatory Design found in the literature. In Case 6, invited keynotes, survey studies on current literature, and steering committee work are vital parts of the work albeit seemingly less participatory when compared to conventional PD activities such as field studies, user workshops or collaborative prototyping. Nevertheless, they are equally important compared to such frontstage activities.

| Level | Authority | Project Activities |
|---|---|---|
| Parliament | Adopts legislations regarding the schools | -- |
| National Agencies | Lays down legislations in executive orders including the overall educational goals | Survey on 21st Century Skills Advisory board participation Multiple lectures on the importance of digital competences |
| Municipalities | Adopts the financial framework, sets local goals, supervises the schools, follows up on results | Keynote on digital divide/digital competence Steering committee partnership Joint applications (EU regional funds) |
| School Committee | Adopts principles for the activities of the school and approves the school budget | FabLab tryout Lectures on the importance of digital competences |
| School | Responsible for the operation of each school makes concrete decisions for the school and regarding individual pupils | Dissemination at a school level Counseling for FabLab establishment Lectures on the importance of digital competences |
| Teacher | Education is characterized by freedom in the choice of method | Observation studies Interventions/experiments Course on digital fabrication 3-day workshop (120 participants) Hands-on workshops Visit to Stanford University |

Figure 7.2: Core Participatory Design activities in FabLab@School relating to the level of authority involved.

The example illustrates that in order to embrace vertical decision making, it may in some cases be important to carry out Participatory Design activities specifically for various levels of decision making. The tools and techniques for doing so may differ for the various levels, the activities need to be carefully planned and executed, and the backstage activities to connect between these activities are important.

At the same time, the case illustrates that Participatory Design projects may involve many groups of stakeholders as users, even though these may not be the actual future users of the specific technology. In order to eventually create a change for the actual future users, the involvement of these vertical levels is important. The vertical processes hence involve stakeholders that need activation in different ways for the different stakeholders.

## 7.5    SUMMARY

In this chapter we addressed the question of how Participatory Design embraces mutual learning and iteration as practical principles of organizing design processes. We have introduced these two as part of four important principles.

We have emphasized that Participatory Design does not mean equal participation of users and designers at all stages in the process and presented methods that help structure and balance the contribution of different stakeholders at different times, with a specific focus on the vertical processes of decision making, typical in particular to governmental and municipal organizations.

Dividing work in the best manners may help plan the design process and bring in the appropriate Participatory Design methods at appropriate times. This also means that Participatory Design activities need to take place at many vertical levels of decision-making which also then involve people as users though they are not and will never be direct users of the technology in question.

**Read More**

We encourage the reader to look at specific methods as mentioned above: the MUST method (Kensing et al., 1996), STEPS (Software Technology for Evolutionary Participatory Systems development) (Floyd et al., 1989), CESD (Grønbæk et al., 1993), and agile contextual design (Beyer, 2010).

CHAPTER 8

# How Does One Get Started on Participatory Design and Stay on Track?

After having presented the activities and toolbox of Participatory Design we will turn to the planning and structuring of a project: how to *initiate*, *implement*, and *navigate* a Participatory Design project. We will offer guiding questions, models, and a compass to scaffold your Participatory Design process. We do that since Participatory Design processes do not come with a complete recipe. Hence, it is important to plan with the resources in the toolbox and the commitments of Participatory Design at hand.

Based on these commitments, the core of planning and carrying out a Participatory Design project is establishing, cultivating, and evaluating a shared goal of completion among designers and users as participants, throughout the entire process from the initial project planning to the final implementation of the Participatory Design outcome. How to put people first is a recurring concern in this chapter. You will learn how to create *a shared goal of completion* with your participants, steer the process through *loops of reciprocal actions*, and evaluate the *degree to which both people and researchers gained* from the Participatory Design process. Finally, we will introduce you to a *Participatory Design compass* that helps you navigate and stay on track through a Participatory Design process. The Participatory Design compass introduces a new set of concepts, such as epistemology and values, that we have not explicitly used so far, but which align very well with the strong commitments emphasized in this book.

## 8.1 GETTING STARTED AS AN HCI STUDENT OR RESEARCHER

Working with people in a Participatory Design process does not differ significantly from other research activities that involve people. It is the responsibility of the researcher, no matter if the researcher is a student, somebody researching at a university, or a researcher/designer in a wider setting, to create a safe environment that follows ethical standards.

These standards may vary from region to region, from state to state, from university to university, or between organizations that the researcher is anchored in. A good place to start planning your Participatory Design projects is to familiarize yourself with standards of your organization, e.g., your local institutional review board (IRB). The institutional review board is, generally speaking, an agency that protects the rights and welfare of human subjects involved in research activities being conducted under its authority, and Participatory Design is one such type of activity. If a Participatory Design project does not fall within such regulations, many of the insights from an IRB protocol can be worth considering to secure the best possible outset for a safe and open collaboration with people in your Participatory Design project.

Based on the purpose of your Participatory Design process, consider the following aspects.

- Who do you want to include and why? What are the criteria for inclusion (profession, age range, gender, language, etc.) that define the participants you plan to include in your Participatory Design process?

- Does the Participatory Design process engage vulnerable people that need extra support?

- What kind of *activities* should be done and which *methods* should be used?

- What are the best *locations* for the Participatory Design process?

- What is the *estimated time* the participants will spend in the project and what is the estimated *duration* of the entire project?

- How does the project secure the privacy and security of the participants, regarding data collection, data analysis, and project dissemination?

- What are the *opt out options* for the participants engaged in the Participatory Design process?

Some questions originating directly from the Participatory Design legacy and commitments (see Chapter 2 and 3) should also be considered.

- What will *people gain* from participating in the project?

- How does the project ensure that people have *equal access to the decisions made* in the Participatory Design process?

- How does the project establish a *friendly and open environment for collaboration*?

- How does the project deal with participants that have *different backgrounds and skills* for engaging with digital technology?

- How do you balance the *power relations* between designers/researchers and users/participants?

- How are Participatory Design *outcomes evaluated and sustained* after the project terminates?

The process of considering these questions is a main concern of the initial stage of a Participatory Design process. However, as the process evolves, the need for revisiting and revising the questions may emerge. The questions (and answers) can be used to navigate the process and revise according to what happens during the process.

## 8.2    WORKING WITH PEOPLE IN PARTICIPATORY DESIGN

The Participatory Design process is a dynamic and dialogical process in which designers and people collectively investigate matters related to the project objectives. Robertson et al. (2014) point to the overall motive of doing Participatory Design, that the design knowledge developed through mutual learning processes leads to better outcomes because of the multiple voices and perspectives engaged in the mutual learning (p. 25). As we saw in Chapter 7, *mutual learning* is as a result an organizing principle of the design process where on one hand, researchers learn from the skillful people in this relation being experts in their everyday or professional practice, and on the other hand, users learn from researchers about novel technologies and new organizing principles. In this way, mutual learning is a motivation, a principle, and an outcome of the Participatory Design process (Kensing and Greenbaum, 2013).

As all other design projects, Participatory Design is most often subject to economic or temporal constraints. PD practitioners often know the duration of a project and the resources available for conducting the Participatory Design process. In the initial stage, it is important to share these constraints and ensure a shared understanding, with users/participants of the project objectives and project plan.

Venturing into a Participatory Design process can be quite different from other more conventional and linear design processes. Where design processes most often have a clear and uncompromisable goal defined by a company, a research group, or a consortium of stakeholders, Participatory Design engages project participants in the process of defining the research question or project outcome. This is partly done in order to have people's perspective included in this initial project stage, and partly to secure ownership and commitment throughout the entire design project. Raising commitment and engagement among people that do neither have a vocabulary for, nor insights into design processes is hence a challenging but very important task, and workshops (Section 5.3) and picture games (Section 6.5) may be used even for this.

## 8.3    A SHARED GOAL OF COMPLETION AND LOOPS OF RECIPROCAL ACTION

So, how do researchers organize their Participatory Design process? Three basic principles apply to most Participatory Design projects. First, the progress of any Participatory Design project is ensured by a *shared goal of completion*. Second, the dynamics of most projects are *loops of reciprocal action* between design team activities and participatory activities. Third, the success of a Participatory Design project is determined by the *degree to which both people and researchers gained* from the participatory design process, which we will discuss further in Section 8.4.

The Participatory Design process is a mutual learning process, but not a symmetrical one between researchers and participants. It is solely the responsibility of the researchers to keep the process running toward the shared end goal, and this includes backstage activities as discussed in Section 7.3. This responsibility is manifested in the dynamics of the Participatory Design process as it unfolds in iterative loops of reciprocal actions between research team activities and participatory activities. Researchers plan for future Participatory Design activities by considering how, when, and by which activities, tools and materials a participatory activity might bring the process forward (see Chapters 5–7). The participatory activity brings about new knowledge to the process that will provide researchers with new inputs for future design and future participatory activities. These are analyzed and interpreted in the design team and thus lead to a new iteration of participatory activities (see Figure 7.1).

## 8.4    THE DEGREE TO WHICH BOTH PEOPLE AND RESEARCHERS GAIN

Participatory Design is an interdisciplinary research field. How researchers frame the goals and objectives of a project depends on, e.g., their disciplinary background. Critical voices in Participatory Design (e.g., Kyng, 1994) argued that the core values and politics of empowerment and democracy often become backgrounded in Participatory Design projects, in favor of a focus on methods and techniques for pragmatic design solutions. As a consequence, some projects tend to focus more narrowly on the activities and artifacts developed through the process, and less on the importance of configuring the process to produce sustainable outcomes and long-term impact on different levels.

In a more holistic Participatory Design perspective, developing digital artifacts to specific contexts and user needs is merely one aspect of a larger context. Empowering people and communities to take part in the development of and decisions concerning their own futures, developing their understanding of the technologies that are embedded in their everyday practices, or creating long-term commitment to changing practices of communities and institutions demands researchers to operate simultaneously at different scales and toward different concerns. As argued by Carroll and Rossen: "*The challenge of participatory design in contemporary community informatics is chiefly one of creating a self-directed and sustainable process of continuous learning*" (2007, p. 258). Hence, participants, both users and researchers, may gain from aspects of the *participatory process*, the *outcomes* (technology, services, systems), and potential *impact or change* of the processes (networks, practices, knowledge) (Smith and Iversen, 2018).

## 8.5    KEEPING THE PARTICIPATORY DESIGN PROJECT ON TRACK

In many design or research processes, milestoning, system requirement lists, or phase models provide a structure for organizing the process and keeping the project on track.

Given the nature of Participatory Design projects, these tools and techniques do not necessarily provide the needed infrastructure to keep the process on track. As argued by Frauenberger et al. (2015), any attempt to retrofit Participatory Design with a (post-)positivist perspective would necessarily make it look scientifically weak, supported by fuzzy data and arbitrary in terms of its conclusions. To help structure the process, we propose a Participatory Design compass that we develop from Frauenberger et al.'s (2015) work on accountability and rigor in Participatory Design. Accountability is understood in terms of linking collaborative work with decisions and outcomes in a transparent way and rigor is understood as internal validity in the process. The compass is a way of navigating the process by asking questions related to values, stakeholders, outcomes, and epistemology.

## 8.6    THE PARTICIPATORY DESIGN COMPASS

The Participatory Design compass brings together four central aspects of a Participatory Design process as "corners" in the model: *Values*, *Stakeholders*, *Outcomes*, and *Epistemology* (see Figure 8.1). Each corner can be used individually or they can all be brought together to conduct a critical and reflective inquiry into a Participatory Design process as it unfolds. Whereas Frauenberger et al. (2015) provide an academic justification and comprehensive account of the compass navigation, we will here emphasize the compass' practical applicability to keep the Participatory Design process on track. Below we present the four corners and relate them to our previous terminology and discussions.

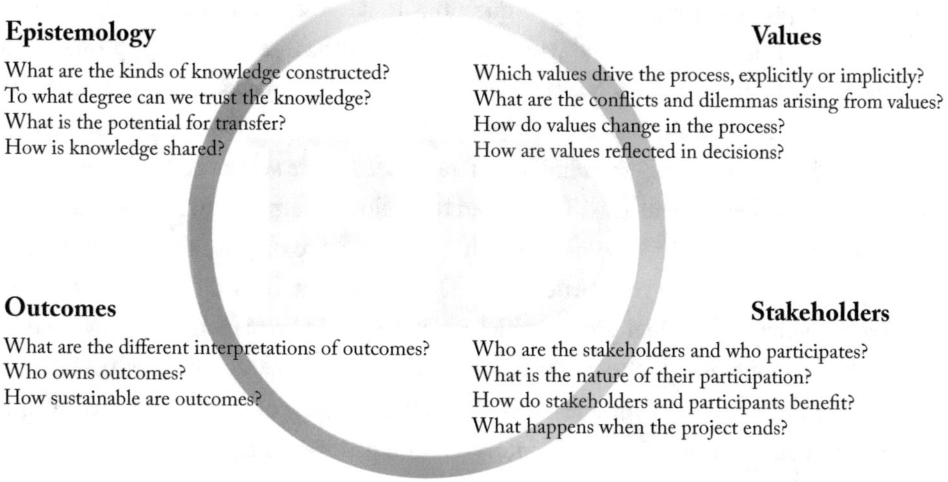

**Epistemology**

What are the kinds of knowledge constructed?
To what degree can we trust the knowledge?
What is the potential for transfer?
How is knowledge shared?

**Values**

Which values drive the process, explicitly or implicitly?
What are the conflicts and dilemmas arising from values?
How do values change in the process?
How are values reflected in decisions?

**Outcomes**

What are the different interpretations of outcomes?
Who owns outcomes?
How sustainable are outcomes?

**Stakeholders**

Who are the stakeholders and who participates?
What is the nature of their participation?
How do stakeholders and participants benefit?
What happens when the project ends?

Figure 8.1: The Participatory Design compass as presented by Frauenberger et al. (2015).

## 8.6.1   VALUES

Iversen et al. (2010) defined values as something beyond that of economic worth and referred to what a person or group of people consider important in life. When working in a mutual learning process, values are seen emerging in the process and not as something that can be unearthed or collected beforehand. In that respect, values are somewhat intangible and abstract, but highly important for understanding how a Participatory Design process develops. Values are both about the general motivation for doing Participatory Design, as they are found in the strong commitments presented earlier, e.g., mutual learning, democracy and skill, and specific values that emerge in collaboration with the stakeholders, as we see in the example in Section 8.7. The values corner of the Participatory Design compass provides a perspective to articulate the values and hence to raise awareness of how values emerge, change, and conflict during the participatory process.

Four questions are essential to pose and continuously work with during the design process.

1. Which values drive the process, explicitly and implicitly?

2. What are the conflicts and dilemmas arising from these values?

3. How do values change in the Participatory Design process?

4. How are values reflected in the decisions?

Iversen and Leong (2012) and Iversen et al. (2012) provided a thorough account of the value perspective in Participatory Design, tracing the cultivation, development, and grounding of values in different Participatory Design projects.

## 8.6.2   STAKEHOLDERS

We started this chapter by emphasizing core questions to address before the Participatory Design process starts. One of them is concerned with stakeholders: What are the criteria for inclusion that define the participants in your Participatory Design process? This question is however an ongoing concern and also not to be decided once and for all: The Participatory Design process may develop in directions in which some (new) stakeholder interests need to be acknowledged more, or become more irrelevant. Frauenberger et al. (2015) provided the following argument: As contexts sometimes diversify or shift, the range of stakeholders equally becomes more diverse, and they bring different motivations, goals, and values to the Participatory Design process. In addition, many Participatory Design projects involve stakeholder groups which are too large to be meaningfully involved in their entirety, and this requires careful choices in terms of representation and means of participation.

Addressing the following four questions allows the diversity of stakeholders to be addressed as a core concern when keeping the Participatory Design process on track.

• Who are the stakeholders and who participates?

- What is the nature of their participation?

- How do stakeholders and participants benefit from the process?

- What happens when the project ends?

### 8.6.3    OUTCOMES

Most design work is for obvious reasons assessed in terms of tangible objects or knowledge production as outcomes. In a Participatory Design process, in which power and authority are shared among the designers and participants, the question of what manifests the design outcome becomes essential.

Three questions scaffold the process of investigating the design outcomes from multiple perspectives.

1. What are the different interpretations of outcomes?

2. Who owns the Participatory Design outcomes?

3. How sustainable are outcomes?

The discussion of Participatory Design outcomes has recently received renewed attention in research. Bratteteig and Wagner (2016) provide a thorough discussion of how we may understand outcomes and Bossen et al. (2018) and Brodersen Hansen et al. (2019) offer a distinction between outputs, outcomes, and impact which can also be utilized as part of the outcome perspective in the four lenses framework. We will return to this topic in Chapter 9.

### 8.6.4    EPISTEMOLOGY

As described by Frauenberger et al. (2015), Participatory Design is a knowledge production process that in many ways differs from classical scientific studies. The epistemology behind Participatory Design is inherently co-constructed, situated, and embodied, like in many other design disciplines but in contrast to what is often seen as scientific knowledge production. Thus, when we use the term *knowledge* in Participatory Design, it is in relation to the kind of insights Participatory Design produces given the situational and contextual constraints of a Participatory Design practice.

Four questions can help expose the fundamental epistemology of a Participatory Design process.

1. What are the kinds of knowledge constructed?

2. To what degree can we trust the knowledge?

3. What is the potential for transfer?

4. How is knowledge shared?

## 8.7   NAVIGATING WITH THE PARTICIPATORY DESIGN COMPASS

The Participatory Design compass is a "tool-to-think-with," guiding designers and researchers in incorporating phases of critical reflection in order to give them a means for navigating the process. The awareness and the language also offer appropriate means to communicate important decisions in the Participatory Design process to the outside world and thus allow researchers/designers to increase the accountability of their choices (Frauenberger et al., 2015).

In our own Participatory Design work, the compass is oftentimes used in situations in which we reflect on our process or our design choices. In the case of the Digital natives project, Case 7, the Participatory Design compass was used on several occasions as a reflection tool to ensure that the young adults were always considered, even when they were not present in the project. In one particular incident, we explicitly used the compass to discard a novel prototype despite the fact that the Participatory Design process was running out of time and resources. Two designers had developed an interactive museum installation in which certain aspects of youth culture were presented. The prototype was novel in its engagement of museum visitors and provided a glimpse of youth culture presented in a very aesthetic way. Nevertheless, we used the questions from the Participatory Design compass to carefully investigate the extent to which the interactive installation responded to the *values* and *stakeholders* perspectives in the Participatory Design process. From the very beginning we had promised the young adults that the exhibition would not be a one-dimensional account of youth culture seen from a grown-up perspective. We also promised them that their viewpoints and concerns counted as much as the museum curators and designers. As the young adults were keen on displaying their own culture as multi-dimensional, emerging and ever changing, these core values simply conflicted with the prototype provided by two designers and the prototype never made it to the final Digital Native exhibition. In this case, the Participatory Design compass was a helpful tool to facilitate dialogues in the Participatory Design process. As in this case, these dialogues can be conflicting and hard.

As Case 7 (the Digital Native case) indicates, the Participatory Design compass helps the inquirers using different perspectives to critically reflect on their work and thereby discover qualities that otherwise would remain tacit.

## 8.8   SUMMARY

In this chapter we described how to initiate, implement, and steer a Participatory Design project based on the core ideals of Participatory Design and using the Participatory Design compass.

Three principles are important when conducting Participatory Design.

1. Establish a shared goal of completion between researchers/designers and users/participants.

2. Plan and reassess throughout the Participatory Design process.

3. Consider the degree to which both users and researchers gained from the Participatory Design process.

Finalizing a Participatory Design project raises concerns for assessing and evaluating its merits both short and long term. This is of particular importance and we have accordingly dedicated Chapter 9 to discuss the outcome of a Participatory Design process and Chapter 10 how to sustain Participatory Design initiatives is an integral part of the Participatory Design process.

**Read More**

There is a rich corpus of Participatory Design literature for getting acquainted with the many nuances of a Participatory Design practice. Luck (2018) provided a good overview of what it is that makes participation in design Participatory Design. The heritage of Participatory Design practice was thoroughly accounted for in Kensing and Greenbaum (2013). Bardzell (2018) interestingly explained how Participatory Design researchers can pursue commitments to social justice and democracy while retaining commitments to reflective practice, the voices of the marginal, and design experiments "in the small". This is not covered in our account above. Many researchers such as Gautam et al. (2018), Bustamante et al. (2018), and Kanstrup and Bertelsen (2016) provided accounts of the circumstances for conducting Participatory Design among vulnerable people. They thoroughly account for the widened responsibility that comes with conducting this kind of participatory practice. The widened responsibility was also emphasized in the work of Spiel et al. (2018). Based on research with vulnerable children, they emphasize the level of micro-ethics in Participatory Design that expands the obligations, responsibilities and practices presented in this chapter. Finally, Bossen et al. (2016a) provided a literature review of how Participatory Design research has evaluated Participatory Design projects over the past three decades. The paper provides an overview of who conducts the evaluation, what is evaluated, and who is engaged in the evaluation over a certain timespan. The paper provides a good starting point for understanding the evaluation practices in Participatory Design research over time.

# PART III

# Participatory Design Results

# CHAPTER 9

# What Are the Results of Participatory Design?

The following three chapters describe how Participatory Design research has matured during the past ten years by focusing on scalability and sustainability of Participatory Design results, and a focus on how the political concerns in Participatory Design have been rekindled. Starting from the four eras of Participatory Design described in Chapter 3, the next chapters focus on the fourth era of Participatory Design and how it has matured.

In this chapter, we address the overarching question of what it is that we produce through Participatory Design. In other words, what is a Participatory Design result? One of the main take-aways from the chapter is that although Participatory Design has been (and still is) particularly concerned with technology, the outcomes of Participatory Design go beyond useful technological products. They may involve organizational change, new practices, insights, learning, or other kinds of effects that reach beyond technology. Moreover, they reflect the four strong commitments in Participatory Design to democracy, empowerment, mutual learning, and skillfulness, as we presented in Chapter 2.

In order to shed light in the nature of Participatory Design results, this chapter will address two sub questions.

1. How can we conceptualize Participatory Design results?

2. How might we evaluate Participatory Design projects and their results?

In addressing these questions, we pick up the thread from the values and gains described in Chapter 5, and the methods and approaches in Chapters 6–8. Some aspects of the questions in focus should be addressed in the initial stages of a project, while others are relevant during the process itself, or toward the end of a project once its outcomes have materialized.

## 9.1  HOW CAN WE CONCEPTUALIZE PARTICIPATORY DESIGN RESULTS?

Despite the somewhat obvious nature of the question, there is no simple answer to what a Participatory Design result is. Looking at the literature, Participatory Design practitioners report results that span from the very tangible and specific, such as a new IT system, to intangible ambitions that take much longer time, such as new organizational structures and democratic influence. Moreover, it is often the case that the results pursued in Participatory Design projects are multifaceted; a project might develop a new technological product but with the long-term ambition of promoting certain values and ideals such as democratization.

## 9.2    A BRIEF HISTORY OF PARTICIPATORY DESIGN RESULTS

Although Participatory Design has been used for many purposes, including the design of organizations and teaching plans, Participatory Design has always been closely tied to the design and introduction of digital technology and their effects. In the early days of Participatory Design, the results pursued ranged from specific technological solutions to be used in workplaces, to educational materials for unions used for technology training and implementation of new working procedures. On an overarching level, the early Participatory Design projects also pursued more grand ideas of democratizing the introduction of technology and empowering skillful workers and unions.

While many of the early projects had explicit goals of creating better technological products, there was also an explicit focus on less tangible results that would help workers and unions gain democratic influence on the technology introduction. As early as 1975, Nygaard and Bergo's report (1975) (related to Case 1) asked what should be considered a result. They suggested that *"results are all actions carried out by the Metal Workers Union (MWU), centrally and locally, which on the basis of activities and insight gained within the project are aiming at giving the MWU and its members increased influence on the planning, control and data processing of the firms"* thus suggesting that "actions" can be considered results. Similarly, Bjerknes et al. (1987) described the explicit focus on technology education for workers and unions which materialized in the production of a significant amount of educational material for unions used for technology training. The background for this focus was the ambition of eventually giving workers a place at the bargaining table (Ibid.). More generally, it could be argued that the core Participatory Design idea of facilitating *mutual learning* (Ehn, 1988; Simonsen and Robertsen, 2012) can be understood as a result. When understanding the design process as an endeavor in which both designers and participants learn new things about their practices and about technology, these learning processes are as such a result of the process. Local knowledge development and democratic influence, both central tenets of early Participatory Design, were explicit and tangible foci for designing quality of products and services (Ehn, 1988) in the Utopia project, Case 2.

How ideals of democracy and participation are reflected in technological products continues to be a concern within Participatory Design (Balka, 2010). Bratteteig and Wagner (2016) more recently took stock of the discussion of Participatory Design results. They explored the nature of a Participatory Design result and discussed how we know if a result is genuinely "participatory" (Bratteteig and Wagner, 2016). They pointed to differences between small and large projects in terms of ambitions and complexities. Big projects address complex issues in a particular domain, spanning across various organizational units and involving multiple stakeholders. Such projects are characterized by domains where work processes are complex and multiple dependencies have to be taken into account, such as healthcare, product development, or manufacturing. Smaller projects may concentrate on problems that are more contained, less ambiguous, and focused, for example, on one specific aspect of a practice or the connection between a few. Such projects typically support one user group or community, and may be planned by a small group of researchers. The smaller projects are easier for researchers to control by, e.g., seeking and creating a dialogue with members of a community and letting those relations develop over time (Ehn et al., 2014). Hence, historically, the context that a Participatory Design project sets up to work within, its boundedness, and the ability of the design team to control or influence key structural aspects are important concerns for achieving a Participatory Design result.

## 9.3    PARTICIPATORY DESIGN INPUTS, PROCESSES, AND EFFECTS

In order to gain some structure in the way we look at Participatory Design results, and to embrace the diverse nature of such results, we will use the terminology adapted from program theory and inspired by Bossen et al. (2018) and Brodersen Hansen et al. (2019). Doing so provides an overarching way of structuring the different kinds of results that may emerge from Participatory Design processes and discussing how they may relate. It is important to note that we are not suggesting that the program theory model can be used as a Participatory Design process model or that it can be used to prescribe particular actions. We use it here simply as a way of structuring the way we think about the kinds of results of Participatory Design.

   In brief, we may distinguish between the inputs, processes and effects of a Participatory Design process. In this chapter, the effects are of particular interest as these represent the various forms of results. *Inputs* refer to the various resources that are mobilized for a project; people, time, technology etc. *Processes* refer to the various activities that are performed during a process. Chapter 5 provides a more detailed account of the kinds of activities of Participatory Design. *Effects* describe the results that emerge from the process in the form of outputs, outcomes and impacts. For our purpose, the distinction between output, outcome and impact allows us to capture the diverse kinds of Participatory Design results and understand how they emerge over time.

## 9.4    PARTICIPATORY DESIGN EFFECTS: OUTPUTS, OUTCOMES, OR IMPACT

In Participatory Design, the *outputs* that emerge from processes involving future users, designers, and stakeholders cover a span from tangible technological artifacts and prototypes, to plans and more intangible outputs such as new ideas (see Chapters 6 and 7). Outputs can be understood as the immediate results that emerge from the process and be directly linked to project activities. While it may obviously be difficult to predict the exact nature and makeup of the output, they are relatively controllable in the sense that they have an immediate link to project activities and can be achieved within the frame of a project. Looking across the Participatory Design literature and history, we can see the diversity of outputs such as the educational material developed in early projects (Bjerknes et al., 1987), healthcare technology, or educational programs (see Chapter 4).

Examples of outputs in the cases are hence, e.g., mock-ups of page layout technologies, or pamphlets to discuss future newspaper production in Case 2, Utopia, prototypes to explore mobile/ on-site planning discussions in Case 8, eGov+, or digital fabrication plans in Case 6, FabLab@ School.

*Outcomes* are not products but the derived benefits, consequences, and drawbacks of what has been done in the process. Outcomes are short- and midterm effects and will develop over time as the artifacts that have been produced or the knowledge developed take effect for the people involved. It may be the case that a new IT system allows people to do their work better or it may provide more work satisfaction. Outcomes are very central to understanding what is unique to Participatory Design. This is because Participatory Design is particularly attuned to the kinds of outcomes that resonate with the four strong commitments presented in Chapter 2. Hence, outcomes often relate to democracy, empowerment, skillfulness, and emancipation. It may be argued that the pursuit of these kinds of outcomes through the use of participatory methods is one of the main things that sets Participatory Design apart from other kinds of design with direct user involvement. The Participatory Design literature gives many examples, from the empowerment of skillful workers in the Utopia project, Case 2, to the democratic ideals of the living labs (Björgvinsson et al., 2010, 2012), and of, e.g., Cases 3, 4, and 7. A series of longitudinal studies in Participatory Design have explored the kinds of outcomes that people enjoy from their participation (Bossen et al., 2010, 2012; Bowen et al., 2013; Garde and Van der Voort, 2014). These show that the outcomes reported by participants (after months to years after their participation) range from new insights and knowledge that shaped participants' professional development, institutional gains in terms of new practices and skillful application of new technology, and a more general new outlook on the role and possibilities of technology.

*Impact* describes long-term effects of an initiative or project. Like outcomes, the kind of impact typically pursued in Participatory Design relates to the strong commitments described in Chapter 2. Impact, however, is difficult to ascribe solely to individual projects as it emerges over extended periods of time and in conjunction with other projects and initiatives. In the early Participatory Design projects (such as Utopia, Case 2), one of the desired impacts was to influence the way in which technology was introduced and designed, promoting skillfulness and influence from workers. These ambitions are evidently not achieved through any single project, but as a desired impact based on sustained engagements. A more recent example is the impact following the FabLab@School project, Case 6, with the introduction of a new K9 course on technology comprehension in the Danish school system. The introduction of this course cannot solely be ascribed to the FabLab@School project and was the product of a range of initiatives and circumstances working in concert, from the classroom floor to the political national level. Similarly, Case 4, 4S, systematically, through its work on open software, has tried to impact technology and the economic forces behind this development. There are indeed many surrounding processes impacting these developments and the long-term effects are hence difficult to foresee. Both cases point to a general issue of evaluating projects in terms of impact, namely that it is difficult to establish causality between individual Participatory Design projects and long-term impacts. Nonetheless, Participatory Design emphasizes the pursuit of and contribution to impacts closely related to the strong commitments described earlier.

## 9.5    FOR WHOM IS IT A RESULT?

A central tenet of Participatory Design is for participants to enjoy lasting results from their participation. But there are potentially many kinds of participants in Participatory Design: future users, management, researchers, designers, technology providers, etc. Taking action on part of the future users of technology has been the most prominent concern in Participatory Design, but there is also reason to acknowledge results that are enjoyed by other stakeholders. Indeed, as described in Chapter 6 under the heading of *infrastructuring*, it is vital to continuously engage with the variety of stakeholders in Participatory Design. In particular, this is important because the more or less formal networks of stakeholders will often play a central role in sustaining results over time (see Chapter 10).

## 9.6    HOW TO EVALUATE PARTICIPATORY DESIGN PROJECTS?

One thing is pursuing Participatory Design results in the form of outputs, outcomes, and impacts, another is determining whether or not these results are actually achieved. This raises the issue of how Participatory Design results may be evaluated. Evaluation has played a surprisingly modest role in Participatory Design's history (Bossen et al., 2016a). Given the fundamentally collaborative nature of Participatory Design, there is good reason to believe that much evaluation is done informally. Nonetheless, the literature does contain principles and examples that show how to evaluate Participatory Design. One of the main challenges stems from the multifaceted nature of Participatory Design results as described above. In other words, what is it more precisely that we are evaluating? Evaluation of technological products is a well known practice in HCI (e.g., Preece et al., 2019) and reflections on how to evaluate products are also found in Participatory Design (Bossen et al., 2016a). So with respect to project completion, Participatory Design research is similar to many other research processes. We evaluate to what extent a project has met its goals. Has any new knowledge been produced and/or did we accomplish a new version or a new artifact as a tangible output from the design process? However, Participatory Design also finds its measures in the outcomes and impact as outlined in the previous section, relating in particular to the strong commitments of Participatory Design. This entails assessing the degree to which the people and organizations engaged in the process gained from their participation.

To get a clearer sense of evaluation in Participatory Design we will discuss two examples which are among the most well-developed in the Participatory Design literature. The first example is conducted by Hertzum and Simonsen (2010), based on their work on health IT. Their evaluations include both quantitative measures of desired effects and qualitative interviews that explore in depth how new IT systems have affected the work of health care professionals. While the methods used are in themselves well known, a notable aspect of Hertzum and Simonsen's work is that the effect measures used for evaluation are co-develop with participants in their project. As such, the evaluation has a distinctly participatory nature as the measures of success are collaboratively developed as part of Participatory Design.

The second example is from Bossen et al. (2010), who provide a retrospective study of what participants gained from their participation. In their study, Bossen et al. interviewed people who had participated in a Participatory Design project exploring the use of technology to create new learning spaces and practices. The interviews were conducted approximately three years after the end of the project. The focus was on understanding what participants had gained personally and professionally as well as the outcomes regarding new teaching practices and ideas. Specifically, the evaluation explored to what extent:

- were people invited to influence the project and product?

- did the process entail any personal gain?

- did the participation lead to more quality of work/life, new possibilities discovered, or more influence on their own work/life conditions?

- did the process provide new areas of competence acquired?

- did participants subsequently experience shifts in career or choice of education, owing to the project?

- did the participants have a new outlook on technology or personal practices?

The two examples demonstrate both the concerns for evaluating the outcomes and impact for the various stakeholders and how evaluation measures can be co-developed with participants, resonating with the ethos of Participatory Design.

## 9.7   SUMMARY

This chapter presented Participatory Design results as three categories of possible effects: outputs that emerge from processes involving future users, designers, and stakeholders cover a span from tangible technological artifacts and prototypes, to plans and more intangible outputs such as new ideas. As opposed to outputs, outcomes are not products but the derived benefits, consequences and drawbacks of what has been done in the Participatory Design process. Finally, impacts describes long-term effects of a Participatory Design project in which also side effects, acts of project "snow-balling" and fundamental new perception of a practice involving new digital technology, is included. The chapter also provides an account of how Participatory Design results are evaluated in relation to the strong commitments of Participatory Design.

**Read More**

Evaluation in Participatory Design can be traced back to at least the 1980's, where Hirschheim (1983) presented results from an interview study involving 20 organizations to assess the merits of "participative" design. Hirschheim, somewhat ironically, found (among other things) that Participatory Design was almost universally praised by participants but was rarely used a second time. The issue of evaluation was picked up again at the first two PDC conferences by Thoresen (1990) and Clement et al. (1992), but in the decades fol-lowing the first two conferences, relatively little attention was given to evaluation. Druin even noted that one of the weaknesses of the Participatory Design literature was the lack of knowledge about formal evaluations. Exceptions include studies by Simonsen and Hert-zum (2008, 2012) and their work on evaluating effects in health care systems. From around 2010, a series of studies re-engaged with the issues of evaluation from the perspective of what users gain from taking part in Participatory Design. In two retrospective studies, Bossen et al. (2010, 2012) explored the long-term gains of users and stakeholders and the potential impediments to these gains. Similar approaches were used by Garde and Van der Vort (2014) and Kapuire et al. (2015) who also applied ongoing activities including focus groups and questionnaires. Among the most comprehensive evaluations is that conducted by Whittle (2014) who explored the relationship between the depth of participation and the outcomes produced. Beyond the evaluations conducted and reported in the literature, several papers propose frameworks and models for how to conduct Participatory Design evaluation. Merkel et al. (2004) argue that that evaluation in Participatory Design should account for long-term and indirect changes in communities and Gerrard and Sosa (2014) present the "PartE" framework consisting of six dimensions and argue the need for a com-mon frame of reference for evaluating and reflecting on Participatory Design projects.

In sum, evaluation can be traced back to the beginning of Participatory Design and has been a recurring issue throughout history. Formal evaluation has, arguably, played a somewhat minor role in Participatory Design but given the nature of discipline there is good reason to believe that both formative and summative evaluation is conducted informally among practitioners.

# CHAPTER 10

# How Does One Sustain Participatory Design Initiatives?

In the previous chapter, we looked at the kinds of results that Participatory Design pursues. One of the main points is that Participatory Design strives to produce outcomes that reach beyond the design of useful and usable products and services and include new ways of working, the development of new communities, increased influence and opportunities, whether in work settings, communities or everyday life. With this ambition follows a concern for how the results of Participatory Design are sustained over time. In other words, how may we ensure that all the ideas, plans and momentum developed during a Participatory Design process are not lost when the project inevitably ends?

In this chapter we address the issue of sustainability in Participatory Design by addressing three questions.

1. What is sustainability in Participatory Design?

2. What are the different conceptions of sustainability?

3. How do you engage with sustainability?

With these topics you will learn how to plan and assess the long-term elements and effects of Participatory Design. This chapter is hence concerned with planning your own departure, and taking a bigger view of the build-up of resources build-up of the project you work with.

## 10.1 WHAT IS SUSTAINABILITY IN PARTICIPATORY DESIGN?

A central tenet for many Participatory Design projects is for participants and organizations to enjoy lasting results. Although many projects are successful in terms of developing new products and working practices and engaging users as a driving force in collaborative design, researchers often (willingly or not) take a leading role in the project. Hence, the sustainability of results is often bound to their presence. However, it is most often the case that the designers or researchers eventually leave the project, because they have to move on, for lack of resources, new research challenges, or for other reasons. If we look, for instance, at the Utopia project, Case 2, this had a strong collaboration between researchers and the graphical workers' unions for several years. Eventually, however, it became necessary for the involved researchers to choose between their research, and a continued engagement with these unions in the role as technology consultants. It is with examples like this in mind that sustainability, and planning for it, are important. The ambition of sustainability as discussed here, is to embrace this concern and make sure that effects and initiatives do not wither and fade when researchers leave.

The concern for *sustainability* has played an important role in Participatory Design's history, as the example shows. Nonetheless, the Participatory Design literature has, until recently, contained relatively few systematic and focused accounts of what sustainability is and how it may be addressed. Recently, Poderi and Dittrich (2018) provided the first systematic review of how sustainability has been addressed in Participatory Design, suggesting that the literature falls in three broad areas: *Participatory Design for sustainability* which is broadly speaking the application of Participatory Design in the interest of pursuing the goals related to sustainability science; *sustainability of Participatory Design practice* addressing how we may ensure the sustained participation of future users and stakeholders throughout the entire process; and finally, the *sustainability of Participatory Design results* that deal with how to ensure lasting results for participants. In this chapter, we are primarily concerned with the latter category. The issues of how participation may be sustained in a Participatory Design process are addressed in Chapters 6 and 8.

It can be argued that the idea of sustainability of Participatory Design results is actually an inherent part of the focus on mutual learning—the idea that all parties learn and develop as part of a design project (Chapters 1, 2, and 9). In this view, participants learn from the project and in this way gain something. There are, however, also more ambitious goals related to sustainability. These relate to sustaining designed services, products or outcomes such as new practices or increased influence. These more explicit concerns for the notion of "sustainability" can be traced back to Clement and van den Besselaar (1993), and possibly further. Clement and aan den Besselaar (1993) pointed to the importance of the participants themselves learning how to take initiative and animate activities at all stages of the design process. Also, they stressed the importance of actors outside of the project knowing and caring about the project, in order for it to achieve lasting results (Ibid.). Carroll et al. (2000) made a similar observation, noting the importance of participants in a long term project changing their roles from informants to analysts, designers and coaches for others in their organization. Carroll et al.'s observations echoes Bødker's proposition (2003), that Participatory Design is not only about project achievements, but about putting the organization in a position where experiences can be used beyond the individual project; in essence, sustainability of project achievements.

## 10.2   DIFFERENT CONCEPTIONS OF SUSTAINABILITY

In terms of what needs to be sustained, Chapter 9 provides a view that distinguishes between outputs, outcomes and impact of Participatory Design. Outputs are generally within the control of the Participatory Design process; project members can design the technological system and collaboratively explore new practices and develop new ideas as part of the proces. Outcomes and impact take time and while they are the central commitments that drive Participatory Design, they are to some extent outside the control of most Participatory Design processes.

Generally, we may ask: More specifically, what needs to be sustained and what do we mean by "sustainability?" In terms of the manifest technological results of Participatory Design (technologies, products, and services) sustainability concerns how to make sure that, e.g., services are maintained and updated over time. If, on the other hand, we look at outcomes such as a new organizational structure or the formation of a community, sustainability reflects a concern for how to make sure that the ideas do not simply fade when researchers or designers leave.

To address sustainability of Participatory Design results, Iversen and Dindler (2008) suggest distinguishing between: *maintaining, scaling, replicating,* and *evolving*. These are not mutually exclusive but can be used to understand or more clearly articulate the ambition of a given project.

- Maintaining points to a strategy in which researchers and participants ensure that the outputs and outcomes of a project do not fade over time, but are kept in place and remain.

- Scaling is a strategy in which an outcome developed in a small project is scaled to a larger context or to include more people, organizational units or communities.

- Replicating is a strategy that is carried out to ensure that results achieved in one place are copied and applied in another situation.

- And finally, evolving as a strategy points out that the effect achieved during a project keeps evolving after the project has ended.

As noted by Kyng (2015), this terminology is based on the notion that 'projects' have a beginning and an end. Looking at Participatory Design history, this is most often the case. However, several authors provide examples of Participatory Design that are not centered on a single "project" but are long-term endeavors where several initiatives and processes are intertwined and represent long and continuous engagement. Kyng (2015) exemplified this with the work with the 4S project, Case 4, which is best understood as a continuous commitment to principles of quality and democracy in healthcare services. This is also the case in Carroll et al.'s (2000) work with communities that stretched over several years and where the work is not necessarily best described as a project. Project or not, the factors and strategies for working with sustainability reported in the literature are similar. In the following section we deal with these factors.

## 10.3   PERSONAL AND PROFESSIONAL NETWORKS

Looking at the Participatory Design literature, a number of ways of engaging are particularly important for the pursuit of sustainability. Broadly speaking, these concern the establishment of personal and professional networks and engagement with different levels of power and authority.

Personal and professional networks, created through Participatory Design, help sustain and further develop the results of Participatory Design. In Chapter 5, we addressed this as a method-ological perspective through infrastructuring. In infrastructuring, as discussed, it is important that participants assume agency and ownership through the process. This helps in implementing, further developing and keeping momentum in project achievements when the project ends.

The common denominator for this strand of literature is the attention to the networks of people and organizations that emerge, the activities that are carried out beyond specific design activities and frontstage work, and how such networks and activities may be nourished to provide the means for sustaining project achievements when a project ends.

Many of the case examples presented earlier have worked specifically with such forms of net-working. The Utopia project, Case 2, made the choice of engaging primarily with graphical workers who were already engaged in networks of union activities, but it also arranged international work-shops where these users, and their unions met with, e.g., journalists and their unions, both at the level of specific newspaper organizations and more generally. These meetings engaged participants in discussions of, e.g., the future division of work in newspapers. Cases 4 (4S), 6 (FabLab@School), 7 (Digital Natives), and 8 (eGov+) all include similar kinds of efforts to formally and informally engage participants across communities, organizations, and organizational units around shared interests (similarly to what Obendorf et al. (2009) call communities of interest).

In Case 8, eGov+, workshops were hosted every six months where municipal workers from the involved professional areas (e.g., local planning) met across the three involved municipalities. In the workshops they participated in structured activities, also together with researchers and product developers from the involved companies, to learn about research results, but more importantly also to share experiences across municipalities.

## 10.4   ENGAGING WITH DIFFERENT LEVELS OF POWER BEYOND THE PROJECT

The importance of engaging with different levels of power and authority pervades the Participa-tory Design. The main rationale is that if a Participatory Design project and its outcomes are to be sustained and potentially scale or develop, political and financial support is needed. Political support may be important in order to drive the agenda, create commitments, and gain legitimacy among other actors so as to secure financial support. Depending on the context, political support may be understood in different ways, whether from politicians or in the context of organizational political processes.

The concern for engaging with different levels of power and actors outside of a project has a long history in Participatory Design. As early as 1996, Gärtner and Wagner discussed how Participatory Design work may play out in different arenas. They identified the level of *the project*, the level of *the organization*, and finally the *national arena*. In this perspective, an important concern is how products and outcomes from the project arena can be scaled to the larger context of an organization or even to a national arena. For this to happen, it is important to mobilize people and resources outside of the project, who have the ability and motivation to scale and communicate project results to actors outside the project. In recent literature, there are several examples of how we may engage in different arenas within Participatory Design. Bødker et al. (2017) showed the importance of engaging with the entire spectrum of power and discussed how different levels of authority play different roles for sustaining and scaling a Participatory Design project, using Case 6 as an example. Moreover, they demonstrated the very different nature of Participatory Design at different levels of power. Where the focus of Participatory Design work is often at the level of the workshop and the direct engagement with future users, Bødker et al. (2017) highlighted the work going into participating in forums with decision makers and national agencies, and the importance of this work to achieve lasting impact of the project. Kyng (2015) provided a complementary perspective by arguing for the need to establish permanent organizational structures to protect participants' interests and maintain democratic control of the results. Figure 7.2 provides an overview of the specific activities at different levels of authority in FabLab@School, Case 6. The case specifically carried out activities at five levels of authority to ultimately address how school children may learn through engaging with so-called FabLabs at school as part of learning about current and future technologies, hence digital empowerment.

The importance of engaging with different levels of authority, power, and actors outside of the project highlights the principle addressed in Chapter 8, namely that it is important to recognize both the frontstage and backstage work of Participatory Design. The literature and the examples provided above concerning the establishing of more or less permanent networks, engagement across arenas, and the establishment of organizational structures address all levels of activities from workshops to collaborative prototyping and infrastructuring work.

## 10.5 WHEN TO DEAL WITH SUSTAINABILITY?

While sustainability concerns may seem to relate primarily to the ending of Participatory Design projects, there is much experience suggesting that engagement with sustainability should start much earlier. Indeed, many Participatory Design projects have a continuous focus on ensuring the sustainability of project achievements once researchers leave. Smith and Iversen (2018) presented a three-dimensional framework for *engagements* to help pursue sustainability throughout the different activities in a Participatory Design process. They emphasized the importance of early engagement with sustainability, including concerns for recruitment of participants and early networking between actors. The early and continuous focus on factors that may support sustainability is also evident in the practices and techniques of Participatory Design. As described in Chapters 6–8, many Participatory Design activities, such as collaborative prototyping, focus on collaboration and the bringing together of diverse stakeholders to find common ground and develop ideas for future technologies and practices. In other words, the collaborative activities performed in Participatory Design do not only serve the purpose of developing ideas together but also of supporting the development of networks, and activities at many levels of power that will eventually prove important in terms of sustainability.

## 10.6  SUMMARY

In this chapter we zoomed in on the growing interest in sustaining Participatory Design results. How do we ensure lasting results for participants? Four different strategies for sustaining Participatory Design were introduced as maintaining, scaling, replicating and evolving Participatory Design results. Sustainability is also a matter of establishing personal and professional networks and engagement with different levels of power and authority from the initial stage of the project. Bringing people together demands a degree of relational expertise, which we suggest is a core competence among Participatory Design researchers and practitioners.

**Read More**

Looking at the Participatory Design literature on sustainability, the importance of personal and professional networks is reflected in several ways. Merkel et al. (2004) noted how personal networks and social relationships within the community provided a crucial infrastructure for sustaining the results of their project. Carroll and Rosson (2007) stressed how strong social networks within communities can support how initiatives from design projects can be carried on. Kaptelinin and Bannon (2012) and Tchounikine (2016) presented ways of considering the connections between the design carried out by designers (externally to the use setting and user community), and the local design carried out by users within their use setting and community of practice. Bossen et al. (2010, 2012) observed that initiatives developed during a Participatory Design project were sustained through networks that stretched across formal organizational boundaries. In an effort to engage with such relations, several authors have used actor-network theory to understand the socio-technical networks and social structures that emerge from design (Gärtner and

Wagner, 1996; DePaula, 2004). Suchman (2002) made the case that design is best understood as entering into already existing networks of working relations and navigating from there. This line of thought is picked up by Light and Akama (2012) who provided detailed accounts of the agency of designers as they are *facilitating* Participatory Design activities. Finally, Dindler and Iversen (2014) suggested that *relational expertise* is in fact a key expertise for Participatory Design practitioners, relational expertise is understood as the capacity of the Participatory Design practitioners to scaffold and nourish the creation of more or less permanent networks within a Participatory Design project. Specifically, Dindler and Iversen (ibid.) used the metaphor of "symbiosis" to describe how the diverse set of actors in a design process may find constellations of mutual benefit.

CHAPTER 11

# Why Is Participatory Design Important Today?

In this book we presented Participatory Design based on our experiences from more than 40 years of Participatory Design research. Our intention is to provide a research-based starting point for bringing Participatory Design to live in future projects, whether at a university or in industry.

We have covered the most frequently asked questions that could restrain you from engaging with Participatory Design in your own work. We have done this with the clear objective of demystifying Participatory Design as a romantic, high church, and inaccessible approach detached from reality. In fact nothing could be more wrong. Participatory Design is a constructive and emphatic way of engaging with people affected by digital technology in their work life, in their social relations or in their private sphere. At the very core, Participatory Design is a genuine ability to engage with people's experiences, challenges and aspirations. It aims to empower people to take an active stance toward the digital technologies that affect their everyday life by offering them a legitimate place for negotiating future technologies. Their possible futures. *It is as simple as that.*

This book has narrowly focused on the Scandinavian Participatory Design approach (the Aarhus version) which is one out of many coexisting research trajectories within the larger corpus of Participatory Design. Diving deeper into the Participatory Design research corpus you can encounter the richness and diversity of Participatory Design as it is practiced around the world and within very different contexts and constraints. Through the years, scholars from various different disciplines have developed, refined and nuanced Participatory Design tools and techniques and ventured into very different domains, all with a profound respect for the people experiencing changes due to digital technology. Other scholars report to the PD community on how Participatory Design is used in more activist ways to empower people in challenging situations on a global scale. Diving into this pool of Participatory Design literature exposes the complexity of working with people in different contexts and life circumstances while maintaining a focus on Participatory Design as a rigorous and accountable research approach. *It is as complex as that.*

When trying to unpack and explain Participatory Design in a relatively accessible manner for people who are not familiar with the tradition, a dilemma emerges. Do you cover as many aspects of Participatory Design as possible at the expense of clarity or do you prioritize clarity and explainability at the expense of nuance? It is not possible to make Participatory Design accessible and clear without losing many nuances, depth, traditions, and even conflicts within Participatory Design research. In this book, our aim has been to make Participatory Design accessible, possibly at the expense of nuance. Participatory Design is, nonetheless, rich in nuance in terms of both research and practice. In this way, this book is *one* account of Participatory Design and its major issues, but it is definitely not the only one.

Emerging challenges within the large scope of humans using technology call for a rethinking of existing Participatory Design approaches and continuous development of approaches for engaging people in the design of future technologies. This calls for attention to the core values and methods of Participatory Design, as well as to a strong research community who is committed to engaging with human and societal challenges. A glance over the recent history of Participatory Design Conferences clearly reveals such aims and ambitions. It shows how Participatory Design can be both committed to its historical and political roots, and expanding to generate a vibrant global community of researchers and practitioners. Following PDC 2014 held in Windhoek, Namibia (see Chapter 4), as the first PDC conference in the Global South, PDC 2016 was held in Aarhus, Denmark. Under the title *Participatory Design in an Era of Participation*, the conference took a critical stance toward the popularized use of "participation" in both academic research and wider society. It focused on bringing back a strong theoretical focus on values, politics and democracy, drawing upon the Scandinavian legacy of Participatory Design. Moreover, efforts were made to expand the interdisciplinary reach of the community further into HCI and related fields of research and practice (Bossen et al., 2016a; Smith et al., 2017). These threads were continued in PDC 2018, in Hasselt and Genk, Belgium, where local municipal elections were brought together with severe global challenges of growing economic and social inequality, migration, under the theme of *Participatory Design, Politics, and Democracy*. The conference questioned both the role of architecture and design practitioners in the participatory processes themselves, and how these can be democratic within a changing political landscape (Huybrechts et al., 2018, Huybrecht and Teli, 2020). The 2020 Participatory Design conference, in Manizales, Colombia, expanded its global reach to South America and to a strong history of political resistance and empowerment of marginalized communities. The title *Participation(s) Otherwise* coined the ambition of bringing together researchers to reflect on the diverse meanings and ontologies that participation and design can take in local and global practices, opening up the understanding of participation beyond modernist narratives and Westernized "universal cookie cutter solutions" (Del Gaudio et al., 2020). Discussions here were fused with the plurality of voices and epistemologies, toward open forms of civic engagement, commons, and alternative (or resistive) technologies and infrastructures. Such trajectories are extended even further in the 2022 edition of PDC, which will be held from Newcastle, UK, as a global hybrid conference around the theme of *Embracing Cosmologies: Expanding the Worlds of Participatory Design* (see https://pdc2022.org).

Within these broader perspectives and (re)interpretations of participation and design we identify the fourth era of Participatory Design, in which we already see several research trajectories as especially interesting in response to emerging challenges. Below we briefly highlight four themes that we believe Participatory Design researchers and practitioners will be engaging with long-term, because of their societal relevance and urgency.

## 11.1    COMMONS

The so-called sharing economy has often been promoted as a way to provide economical alternatives and bottom-up initiatives, yet it is also tightly connected with construction of technological platforms that can be marketed and made money from (Uber, AirBnB, etc.). Many local communities at the same time struggle to find and use cheap/free technologies without aspiration to make money, making the most with the possibilities they have. Commonfare, Case 3, (as we have presented earlier) is one example of a project that aims for such alternatives (see also, e.g., Platform Cooperatives https://en.wikipedia.org/wiki/Platform_cooperative).

The notions of commons and commoning are currently debated in the Participatory Design community to focus on alternative ways of organizing society toward more social, ecological, and sustainable forms. Commons as forms of organizing rely on communication, awareness and self-regulation among the contributors in contrast to central control and private ownership (see, e.g., Sciannamblo et al., 2021; Botero et al., 2020; Marttila et al., 2014; Teli, 2015)

Commons is hence one of the ways that we currently see where it is possible and important to work locally and practically with people, and where Participatory Design has a role to play. At the same time this arena raises interesting societal and political challenges qua the potential of rethinking and reframing of ownership over technological solutions and design processes as well as of the societal infrastructures at various scales including those of government and political decision making.

## 11.2    DECOLONIZATION AND PLURALITY

An important concern that has been brought out of Participatory Design research in recent years is: Whose future(s) are we concerned with? Many forms of concerns have been raised regarding race, structural inequality, the reproduction of poverty and marginalization in addition to global health crises such as the COVID-19 pandemic. In the Participatory Design literature and conferences, we have seen recent emphasis on decolonization and a move toward pluriversality (eg. Del Gaudio et al., 2020; Arruda et al., 2020; Szaniecki et al., 2020; Smith et al., 2021): New waves from the Global South have been critical to, but also suggested the possibility to infuse, Scandinavian or Western orientations to Participatory Design. As argued by Smith et al. (2020a), conventional Participatory Design approaches seem particularly well suited to contribute to debates over power and decolonization in design, yet often lack considerations of cultural situatedness and underlying ontological entanglements. Recent efforts to explore theoretical and methodological gaps in Participatory Design relating to contemporary discourses of decolonizing design is an important aspect of inclusive and globally relevant forms of Participatory Design.

These attempts leave important questions for further elaboration and debate, framed as *inclusive futures*: How mainstream or how radical will our approaches need to become in order to cater sufficiently for diverse groups of citizens and communities? How may our approaches cater for conflict and diversity between various needs and perspectives?

## 11.3   SUSTAINING TECHNOLOGY

We have elsewhere (Chapter 10) talked at length about sustainability of processes and outcomes. A central concern is how the next generation of citizens will be able to meaningfully deal with the rapid digitalization and impact of emergent technologies? What new literacies are needed for educating and empowering future generations, institutions, and organizations, in the face of societal digitalization? In our own research we have identified the need to support the ability on individual and community levels to determine the potential impact on emerging technologies. This is a move from computational thinking to computational empowerment (Iversen et al., 2018; Dindler et al., 2020), focusing on necessary competences for future generations to understand and construct with digital technologies. It is necessary to support this ability on individual and group levels to determine and work with the potential impact of digital and emerging technologies (DiSalvo et al., 2017). Hence, such future competencies must embrace not only use of such technologies but also design, construction and critical reflection on their impact.

This engagement is necessary at the level of society and citizenship, but also still for work and the workplace. As in the days of Nygaard (Nygaard and Bergo, 1975; Kaasbøl, 1983), designers needed to support the end-users' ability to participate in the decision making processes that impact both the agency and control of the work of their colleagues and institutions. For the next generation of future designers, design competences are changing in line with increasing impact and complexity of technologies in society. Researchers and industry are calling for future designers to have a broader range of competences; from insights into data modeling and algorithmic design, to more classic interface and interaction design, to the ethical, political, and societal implications of technologies and values that Participatory Design should seek to address.

## 11.4   RESPONSIBLE DATA

In addition to the above three challenges that are part of current Participatory Design research, data is one area where we believe Participatory Design as a research approach could offer valuable potential.

How do we provide people with the knowledge, tools, and organizations needed to make informed and ethical decisions about their personal data? In the CSCW 2020 keynote, Afua Bruce from DataKind, a "nonprofit organization on a mission to harness the power of data science in the service of humanity" presented her analyses of successful real-world projects. She identified components of high impact, successful data for good programs and pointed toward challenges of civic engagement, best practices for ethical AI, and co-designing inclusive projects. These experiences have strong parallels to the challenges of Participatory Design and it seems that data science, when brought out of the realms of profit, could be an area that could benefit from fruitful co-existence with Participatory Design (Bratteteig and Verne, 2018; Loi et al., 2018; Choi et al., 2020)

The use of predictive technologies in public institutions is one example where both citizens and caseworkers are confronted with a new lack of transparency, explainability and control of systems. The field of HCI at large has tried to embrace these challenges (see Abdul et al., 2018) and it is our suggestion that Participatory Design has important roles to play, by engaging designers, researchers, and citizens in exploring future relations between humans and machines. Caselli et al. (2021) engage with a case of communities, data and Natural Language Processing, and point out that an important challenge is that data and communities are not separate, and that none of them are static, hence arguing for the relevance of Participatory Design. Many other new research initiatives focus on harnessing the human aspects of emerging technologies, and AI in particular. Such initiatives can benefit from strong alliances with PD researchers to promote genuine empowerment, diversity and democracy through citizen and institutional engagement. The CPSR Computer Professionals for Social Responsibility has recently been revived in the context of PDC and CSCW 2020 (see Becker et al., 2020). Such initiatives will provide collective forums and activist alliances for social responsibility in the future of computing that reinvigorate Participatory Design's political values from its early history, and provide new meaning for an increasingly digitalized future.

## 11.5 THE STRONG COMMITMENTS OF PARTICIPATORY DESIGN ARE MORE IMPORTANT THAN EVER

If you have not already asked yourself the question, now is the time: What use to make of a design tradition rooted in the 1970's Scandinavian labor market in a global digitized world?

With reference to our definition of Participatory Design in Chapter 1, we have throughout this book described Participatory Design as four strong commitments.

1. Participatory Design is committed to *democracy*, at the workplace and beyond.

2. Participatory Design is concerned with the *empowerment* of people through the *processes of design*.

3. Participatory Design aims for *emancipatory practices* rooted in *mutual learning* between designers and people.

4. Fundamentally this is done by seeing human beings as *skillful* and *resourceful* in the development of their *future practices*.

Fifty years after the first Participatory Design projects emerged in Scandinavia, these strong commitments are still relevant and important on a global scale, as they attempt to secure a respectful understanding of how digital technologies influence people, practices, and societies by *putting people first* in the design and implementation of new digital technology. This doctrine—putting people first in design—is perhaps even more important today as rapid digitalization influences the basic infrastructures in our contemporary society. Let us elaborate on that.

Whereas digitalization of our societies is undoubtedly important and with great potential, digital technologies are causing an increase in inequality between people and cultures, threats of eroding our democratic rights, a lack of ethical concerns in the development of artificial intelligence and exploitation of data that infringe on our privacy and digital security as individuals and communities. We have pointed to a few of the challenges above, such as increased socio-economic inequality, colonization and unethical data-usage. In the light of such challenges, Participatory Design and its strong commitments to engage people in the process of designing their future technologies, is one way to secure a conscientious digitalization that takes the point of departure in people and their life-worlds.

To put it simply, Participatory Design can deliver the grounding perspective, methods, tools, and techniques needed for bringing people, quality of life, and democracy back to the center of the design of digital technology. We encourage researchers and designers to explore the potential of giving people a voice in the design process and to pursue the strong commitments of Participatory Design, contributing to the ever-evolving knowledge in this people-centric design tradition. You are more than welcome here.

# Bibliography

Ashraf Abdul, Jo Vermeulen, Danding Wang, Brian Y. Lim, and Mohan Kankanhalli. 2018. Trends and trajectories for explainable, accountable and intelligible systems: An HCI research agenda. In *Proceedings of the 2018 CHI Conference on Human Factors in Computing Systems (CHI '18)*. Association for Computing Machinery, New York, NY, Paper 582, pp. 1–18. DOI: 10.1145/3173574.3174156. 115

Katerina Ananiadoui and Magdalean Claro. 2009. 21st century skills and competences for new millennium learners in OECD countries, *OECD Education Working Papers*, No. 41, OECD Publishing, Paris, DOI:10.1787/218525261154. 38

Antonella De Angeli, Silvia Bordin, and Maria Menendez Blanco. 2014. Infrastructuring participatory development in information technology. *Proceedings of the 13th Participatory Design Conference*. DOI: 10.1145/2661435.2661448. 45

Marcella Arruda, Michael Haldrup, and Kristine Samson. 2020. Performing citizenship through design? In *Proceedings of the 16th Participatory Design Conference 2020—Participation(s) Otherwise*. Manizales, Colombia, 2: pp. 59–62. DOI: 10.1145/3384772.3385139. 113

Mara Balestrini, Yvonne Rogers, and Paul Marshall. 2015. Civically engaged HCI: tensions between novelty and social impact. In *Proceedings of the 2015 British HCI Conference (British HCI '15)*. ACM, New York, NY, pp. 35–36. DOI: 10.1145/2783446.2783590. 71

Ellen Balka. 2010. Broadening discussion about participatory design: A reply to Kyng. *Scandinavian Journal of Information Systems* 22(1) Article 7. 96

Stinne Aaløkke Ballegaard, Thomas Riisgaard Hansen, and Morten Kyng. 2008. Healthcare in everyday life: designing healthcare services for daily life. In *Proceedings of the SIGCHI Conference on Human Factors in Computing Systems (CHI '08)*. ACM, New York, NY, pp. 1807–1816. DOI: 10.1145/1357054.1357336. 32

Liam Bannon, Jeffrey Bardzell, and Susanne Bødker. 2018a. Introduction: Reimagining participatory design—emerging voices. *ACM Transactions Computer-Human Interactions* 25(1) Article 1 (February 2018), 8 pages. DOI: 10.1145/3177794. xvii, xviii, 24, 29, 46

Liam Bannon, Jeffrey Bardzell, and Susanne Bødker. 2018b. Reimagining participatory design. *Interactions* 26(1): pp. 26–32. DOI: 10.1145/3292015. xviii, 29

Liam Bannon. 1991. From human factors to human actors: The role of psychology and human-computer interaction studies in system design. In *Design at Work: Cooperative Design of Computer Systems*, J. Greenbaum and M. Kyng, Eds. Erlbaum, pp. 25–44. DOI: 10.1201/9781003063988-3. 6, 20

Chiara Bassetti, Mariacristina Sciannamblo, Peter Lyle, Maurizio Teli, Stefano De Paoli, and Antonella De Angeli. 2019. Co-designing for common values: creating hybrid spaces to nurture autonomous cooperation, *CoDesign* 15(3): pp. 256–271, DOI: 10.1080/15710882.2019.1637897. 26

Shaowen Bardzell. 2018. Utopias of pParticipation: Feminism, design, and the futures. *ACM Transactions Computer-Human Interactions* 25(1), Article 6 (February 2018), 24 pages. DOI: 10.1145/3127359. 91

Christopher Becker, Ann Light, Christopher Frauenberger, Dawn Walker, Victoria Palacin, Syed Ahmed, Rachel C. Smith, Pedro Cuellar, and David Nemer. 2020. Computing professionals for social responsibility: The past, present and future values of participatory design. In *Proceedings of the 16th Participatory Design Conference 2020-Participation (s) Otherwise* 2: pp. 181–184. DOI: 10.1145/3384772.3385163. 115

Miriam Begnum and Therese Thorkildsen. 2015. Comparing user-centered practices in agile versus non-agile development, *Nokobit* 23(1). http://ojs.bibsys.no/index.php/Nokobit/article/view/270. 77

Tilde Bekker, Julie Beusmans, David Keyson, and Peter Lloyd. 2003. KidReporter: a user requirements gathering technique for designing with children. *Interacting with Computers* 15(2): pp. 187–202. DOI: 10.1016/S0953-5438(03)00007-9. 37, 45, 56

Steve Benford, Benjamin B. Bederson, Karl-Petter Åkesson, Victor Bayon, Allison Druin, Pär Hansson, Juan Pablo Hourcade, Rob Ingram, Helen Neale, Claire O'Malley, Kristian T. Simsarian, Danaë Stanton, Yngve Sundblad, and Gustav Taxén. 2000. Designing storytelling technologies to encouraging collaboration between young children. In *Proceedings of the SIGCHI Conference on Human Factors in Computing Systems (CHI '00)*. ACM, New York, NY, pp. 556–563. DOI: 10.1145/332040.332502. 68

David Benyon. 2013. *Designing Interactive Systems: A Comprehensive Guide to HCI, UX and Interaction Design*. Pearson Education (First edition with Phil Turner and Susan Turner 2005). 2, 21

Olav Bertelsen, Kim Halskov, Shaowen Bardzell, and Ole Sejer Iversen. 2015. *Proceedings of The Fifth Decennial Aarhus Conference on Critical Alternatives*. Aarhus University Press, Aarhus N. DOI: 10.7146/aahcc.v1i1.22349. 29

Olav Bertelsen, Niels Olof Bouvin, Peter Krogh, and Morten Kyng. 2005. *Proceedings of the 4th Decennial Conference on Critical Computing: Between Sense and Sensibility*. ACM, New York, NY. 28

Hugh Beyer. 2010. User-centered agile methods. *Synthesis Lectures on Human-Centered Informatics*. DOI: 10.2200/S00286ED1V01Y201002HCI010. 76, 77, 82

Thomas Binder, Judith Gregory, and Ina Wagner. 2002. Introduction, *PDC Proceedings*, CPSR. 22

Gro Bjerknes and Tone Bratteteig. 1987. Florence in wonderland: system development with nurses. In: G. Bjerknes, P. Ehn, and M. Kyng, Eds., *Computers and Democracy*, Erlbaum. 17, 31, 45

Gro Bjerknes and Tone Bratteteig. 1995. User participation and democracy: A discussion of Scandinavian research on system development. *Scandinavian Journal of Information Systems* 7.1: 1. 51

Gro Bjerknes, Pelle Ehn, and Morten Kyng (Eds). 1987. *Computers and Democracy—a Scandinavian Challenge*. Gower Publishing. 28, 61, 96, 98

Erling Björgvinsson, Pelle Ehn, and Per-Anders Hillgren. 2010. Participatory design and "democratizing innovation". In *Proceedings of the 11th Biennial Participatory Design Conference (PDC'10)*. ACM, New York, NY, pp. 41–50. DOI: 10.1145/1900441.1900448. 98

Erling Björgvinsson and Per-Anders Hillgren. 2004. On the spot experiments within healthcare. In *Proceedings of the Eighth Conference on Participatory Design: Artful Integration: Interweaving Media, Materials and Practices* 1 (PDC 04). ACM, New York, NY, pp. 93–101. DOI: 10.1145/1011870.1011882. 32, 45

Erling Björgvinsson, Pelle Ehn, and Per-Anders Hillgren. 2012. Agonistic participatory design: Working with marginalized social movements. *CoDesign* 8: pp. 2–3, 2012. DOI: 10.1080/15710882.2012.672577. 43, 98

Wolf-Gideon Bleek, Martti Jeenicke, and Ralf Klischewski. 2002. Developing web-based applications through e-prototyping. In *Proceedings of the 26th International Computer Software and Applications Conference on Prolonging Software Life: Development and Redevelopment (COMPSAC '02)*, pp. 609–614. 57

Jeanette Blomberg and Helena Karasti. 2012. Positioning ethnography within Participatory Design. In *Routledge International Handbook of Participatory Design*, J. Simonsen and T. Robertson, Eds., Routledge, London, pp. 86–116. 51, 52

Susanne Bødker and Ellen Christiansen. 1997. Scenarios as springboards in design. In G. Bowker, L. Gasser, S. L. Star, and W. Turner, Eds., *Social Science Research, Technical Systems and Cooperative Work*, pp. 217–234. Erlbaum.

Susanne Bødker and Ellen Christiansen. 2004. Designing for ephemerality and prototypicality. In *Proceedings of the 5th Conference on Designing Interactive Systems: Processes, Practices, Methods, and Techniques (DIS '04)*. ACM, New York, NY, pp. 255–260. DOI: 10.1145/1013115.1013151. 57, 67, 76

Susanne Bødker and Kaj Grønbæk. 1991a. *Design in Action: From Prototyping by Demonstration to Cooperative Prototyping*. Lawrence Erlbaum Associates, pp. 197–218. DOI: 10.1201/9781003063988-12. 8, 12, 56, 57, 67

Susanne Bødker and Kaj Grønbæk. 1991b. Cooperative prototyping: users and designers in mutual activity. *International Journal of Man-Machine Studies* 34(3): pp. 453–478. Academic Press. DOI: 10.1016/0020-7373(91)90030-B. 56, 57, 67, 71

Susanne Bødker and Morten Kyng. 2018. Participatory design that matters—facing the big issues. *ACM Transactions on Computer-Human Interaction* 25(1): pp. 1–30. DOI: 10.1145/3152421. xviii, 18, 24, 32, 33

Susanne Bødker and Ole Sejer Iversen. 2002. Staging a professional participatory design practice: moving PD beyond the initial fascination of user involvement. In *Proceedings of the Second Nordic Conference on Human-Computer Interaction (NordiCHI '02)*. ACM, New York, NY, pp. 11–18. DOI: 10.1145/572020.572023. 3

Susanne Bødker and Pär-Ola Zander. 2015. Participation in design between public sector and local communities. In *Proceedings of the 7th International Conference on Communities and Technologies (C&T'15)*. ACM, New York, NY, pp. 49–58. DOI: 10.1145/2768545.2768546. xviii, 40, 45, 80

Susanne Bødker and Yngve Sundblad. 2007. Usability and interaction design—new challenges for the Scandinavian tradition. *Behavior and Information Technology* 27(4): pp. 293–300. DOI: 10.1080/01449290701760682. 67

Susanne Bødker, Christian Dindler, and Ole Sejer Iversen. 2017. Tying knots: Participatory infrastructuring at work. *Computer Supported Cooperative Work* 26(1–2): pp. 245–273. DOI: 10.1007/s10606-017-9268-y. xviii, 8, 39, 75, 76, 78, 80, 81, 107

Susanne Bødker, Christian Dindler, Kim Halskov, and Ole Sejer Iversen. 2016. Advances in participatory design. In *CHI EA '16: Proceedings of the 2016 CHI Conference Extended Abstracts on Human Factors in Computing Systems*, ACM, pp. 984–987. DOI: 10.1145/2851581.2856688. xv

Susanne Bødker, Pelle Ehn, John Kammersgaard, Morten Kyng, and Yngve Sundblad. 1987. *A Utopian Experience: On Design of Powerful Computer-Based Tools for Skilled Graphic Workers.*

*Computers and Democracy—A Scandinavian Challenge*, G. Bjerknes, P. Ehn, and M. Kyng, Eds., Gower Publishing Ltd., pp. 251–278. 17, 28

Susanne Bødker, Pelle Ehn, Staffan Romberger, and Dan Sjögren. 1985. *The UTOPIA Project: An Alternative in Text and Images (Graffiti 7)*. Swedish Center for Working Life. 17, 20

Susanne Bødker. 1990. *Through the Interface: A Human Activity Approach to User Interface Design*. L. Erlbaum Associates Inc., Hillsdale, NJ. 28

Susanne Bødker. 1993. The AT-project: Practical research in cooperative design. *DAIMI Report Series* 22: p. 454. DOI: 10.7146/dpb.v22i454.6772. 45, 68

Susanne Bødker. 1996. Creating conditions for participation: Conflicts and resources in systems development, *Human-Computer Interaction* 11: pp. 215–236. DOI: 10.1207/s15327051hci1103_2. 60, 76

Susanne Bødker. 2003. A for alternatives, *Scandinavian Journal of Information Systems*, 15(1), Article 1. Available at: http://aisel.aisnet.org/sjis/vol15/iss1/1. 3, 37, 104

Susanne Bødker. 2006. When second wave HCI meets third wave challenges. *Proceedings of the 4th Nordic Conference on Human-Computer Interaction: Changing Roles*. ACM, New York, pp. 1–8. DOI: 10.1145/1182475.1182476. 45

Susanne Bødker. 2015. Third-wave HCI, 10 years later—participation and sharing. *Interactions* 22(5) (September–October 2015): pp. 24–31. DOI: 10.1145/2804405. 45

Morten Bohøj, Nikolaj Borchorst, Matthias Korn, Susanne Bødker, and Pär-Ola Zander. 2011. Public deliberation in municipal planning: Supporting action and reflection with mobile technology. *Proceedings of Communities and Technologies' 11*. pp. 88–97. DOI: 10.1145/2103354.2103367. xviii, 40, 41, 45, 55, 68, 69, 70

Morten Bohøj, Nikolaj Borchorst, Niels Olof Bouvin, Susanne Bødker, and Pär-Ola Zander. 2010. Timeline collaboration. *Proceedings of CHI'10*. ACM, New York, pp. 523–532. DOI: 10.1145/1753326.1753404. 40, 45

Per Erik Boivie. 2007. *Global Standard—How Computer Displays Worldwide Got The TCOLogo*, Premiss. 17

Peter Börjesson, Wolmet Barendregt, Eva Eriksson, and Olof Torgersson. 2015. Designing technology for and with developmentally diverse children: a systematic literature review. In *Proceedings of the 14th International Conference on Interaction Design and Children (IDC '15)*. ACM, New York, NY, pp. 79–88. DOI: 10.1145/2771839.2771848.

Marcel Borowski, Roman Rädle, and Clemens N. Klokmose. 2018. Codestrate packages: An alternative to "one-size-fits-all" software. In *Extended Abstracts of the 2018 CHI Conference on Human Factors in Computing Systems (CHI EA '18)*. ACM, New York, NY, Paper LBW103, pp. 1–6. DOI: 10.1145/3170427.3188563. 70

Claus Bossen, Christian Dindler, and Ole S. Iversen. 2010. User gains and PD aims: assessment from a participatory design project. In *Proceedings of the 11th Biennial Participatory Design Conference (PDC '10)*, pp. 141–150. DOI: 10.1145/1900441.1900461. 62, 98, 100, 108

Claus Bossen, Christian Dindler, and Ole S. Iversen. 2016a. Evaluation in participatory design: a literature survey. In *Proceedings of the 14th Participatory Design Conference: Full Papers - Volume 1 (PDC '16)*, pp. 151–160. DOI: 10.1145/2940299.2940303. xviii, 91, 99, 112

Claus Bossen, Christian Dindler, and Ole Sejer Iversen. 2012. Impediments to user gains: experiences from a critical participatory design project. In *Proceedings of the 12th Participatory Design Conference: Research Papers 1 (PDC '12)*. ACM, New York, NY, pp. 31–40. DOI: 10.1145/2347635.2347641. 98, 108

Claus Bossen, Christian Dindler, and Ole Sejer Iversen. 2018. Program theory for participatory design. In *Proceedings of the 15th Participatory Design Conference: Short Papers, Situated Actions, Workshops and Tutorial, 2 (PDC '18)*. ACM, New York, NY, Article 3, pp. 1–4. DOI: 10.1145/3210604.3210638. 89, 97

Claus Bossen, Rachel Charlotte Smith, Anne Marie Kanstrup, Janet McDonnell, Maurizio Teli, and Keld Bødker. 2016b. *Proceedings of the 14th Participatory Design Conference: Full Papers 1*. ACM, New York, NY. 29

Claus Bossen. 2006. Participation, power, critique: constructing a standard for electronic patient records. In *Proceedings of the Ninth Conference on Participatory Design: Expanding Boundaries In Design 1 (PDC '06)*. ACM, New York, NY, pp. 95–104. DOI: 10.1145/1147261.1147276. 32, 45

Andrea Botero, Sanna Marttila, Giacomo Poderi, Joanna Saad-Sulonen, Anna Seravalli, Maurizio Teli, and Frederick M.C van Amstel. 2020. Commoning design and designing commons. In *Proceedings of the 16th Participatory Design Conference 2020 - Participation(s) Otherwise 2*. ACM, New York, NY, pp. 178–180. DOI: 10.1145/3384772.3385162. 113

Niels Olof Bouvin, Christina Nielsen, and Christian Sejersen. 1996. Spirits in a material world. Thesis, Computer Science, Aarhus University. 68

Simon Bowen, Kerry McSeveny, Eleanor Lockley, Dan Wolstenholme, Mark Cobb, and Andy Dearden. 2013. How was it for you? Experiences of participatory design in the UK health service. *CoDesign* 9(4): pp. 230–246. DOI: 10.1080/15710882.2013.846384. 98

Jørn Braa and Sundeep Sahay. 2012. Health information systems program: Participatory design within the HISP network. In *Routledge International Handbook of Participatory Design*, J. Simonsen and T. Robertson, Eds., Routledge, pp. 235–256. 32, 45

Jørn Braa, Ola Hodne Titlestad, and Johan Sæbø. 2004. Participatory health information systems development in Cuba: the challenge of addressing multiple levels in a centralized setting. In *Proceedings of the Eighth Conference on Participatory Design: Artful Integration: Interweaving Media, Materials and Practices* 1. ACM, New York, NY, pp. 53–64. DOI: 10.1145/1147261.1147271. 32, 45

Eva Brandt, and Camilla Grunnet. 2000. Evoking the future: Drama and props in user centered design. In *Proceedings of the Participatory Design Conference (PDC '00)*, pp. 11–20. 56

Eva Brandt. 2006. Designing exploratory design games: a framework for participation in Participatory Design?. In *Proceedings of the Ninth Conference on Participatory Design: Expanding Boundaries in Design* 1: pp. 57–66. DOI: 10.1145/1147261.1147271. 56

Tone Bratteteig and Guri Verne, 2018. Does AI make PD obsolete? Exploring challenges from artificial intelligence to participatory design. *Proceedings of the 15th Participatory Design Conference: Short Papers, Situated Actions, Workshops and Tutorial*, 2. DOI: 10.1145/3210604.3210646. 115

Tone Bratteteig and Ina Wagner. 2016. What is a participatory design result?. In *Proceedings of the 14th Participatory Design Conference: Full papers* 1: pp. 141–150. DOI: 10.1145/2940299.2940316. 76, 89, 96

Tone Bratteteig, Keld Bødker, Yvonne Dittrich, Preben Holst Mogensen, and Jesper Simonsen. 2013. Methods: organizing principles and general guidelines for Participatory Design projects. *Routledge International Handbook of Participatory Design*.1st Edition. p. 28. 76

Ulrich Briefs, Claudio U. Ciborra, and Leslie Schneider. 1982. Systems design for, with, and by the users, *Proceedings of the IFIP WG 9.1 Working Conference on Systems Design For, With, and by the Users*, Riva Del Sole, Italy, pp. 20–24 September 1982. 27

Ana Bustamante Duarte, Nina Brendel, Auriol Degbelo, and Christian Kray. 2018. Participatory design and participatory research: An HCI case study with young forced migrants. *ACM Transactions on Computer-Human Interaction* 25(1): pp. 1–39. DOI: 10.1145/3145472. 46, 91

Jacob Buur and Astrid Søndergaard. 2000. Video card game: an augmented environment for user centered design discussions. In *Proceedings of DARE 2000 on Designing Augmented Reality environments (DARE '00)*, pp. 63–69. DOI: 10.1145/354666.354673. 72

John M. Carroll and Mary Beth Rosson. 2007. Participatory design in community informatics. *Design Studies* 28: pp. 243–261. DOI: 10.1016/j.destud.2007.02.007. 42, 61, 86, 108

John M. Carroll, George Chin, Mary Beth Rosson, and Dennis C. Neale. 2000. The development of cooperation: Five years of participatory design in the virtual school. In *Proceedings of the 3rd Conference on Designing Interactive Systems: Processes, Practices, Methods, and Techniques (DIS '00)*. ACM, New York, NY, pp. 239–251. DOI: 10.1145/347642.347731. 101, 105

John M. Carroll. 2000. *Making Use: Scenario-Based Design of Human-Computer Interactions*. MIT Press. DOI: 10.1145/347642.347652. 51

Tommaso Caselli, Roberto Cibin, Costanza Conforti, Enrique Ecinas, and Maurizio Teli. 2021. Guiding principles for participatory design-inspired natural language processing. *Proceedings of the 1st Workshop on NLP for Positive Impact*. Association for Computational Linguistics, pp. 27–35. DOI: 10.18653/v1/2021.nlp4posimpact-1.4. 115

Tim Cederman-Haysom and Margot Brereton. 2006. A participatory design agenda for ubiquitous computing and multimodal interaction: a case study of dental practice. In *Proceedings of the Ninth Conference on Participatory Design: Expanding Boundaries in Design* 1: pp. 11–20. DOI: 10.1145/1147261.1147264. 57

Bo T. Christensen, Kim Halskov, and Clemens N. Klokmose, Eds. 2020. *Sticky Creativity. Post-it Note Cognition, Computers, and Design*. Academic Press. 72

Henrik Bærbak Christensen, Klaus Marius Hansen, Morten Kyng, and Konstantinos Manikas. 2014. Analysis and design of software ecosystem architectures, toward the 4S telemedicine ecosystem, *Information and Software Technology* 56(11): pp. 1476-1492, DOI: 10.1016/j.infsof.2014.05.002, http://www.sciencedirect.com/science/article/pii/S0950584914001050. 33

Jaz Hee-jeong Choi, Laura Forlano, and Denisa Kera. 2020. Situated automation: Algorithmic creatures in participatory design. In *Proceedings of the 16th Participatory Design Conference 2020 - Participation(s) Otherwise*, Manizales, Colombia, 2: pp. 5–9, ACM. DOI: 10.1145/3384772.3385153. 115

Andrew Clement and Peter Van den Besselaar. 1993. A retrospective look at PD projects. *Communications of the ACM* 36(6): pp. 29–37. DOI: 10.1145/153571.163264. 17, 104

Andrew Clement and Peter van den Besselaar. 2004. *Proceedings of the Eighth Conference on Participatory Design: Artful Integration: Interweaving Media, Materials and Practices* 1. ACM, New York, NY. 22

Andrew Clement, Marc Griffiths, and Peter van den Besselaar. 1992. *Participatory Design Projects: A Retrospective Look*. PDC 1992. 101

Alistair Cockburn. 2001. *Writing Effective Use Cases*. Addison-Wesley. 77

Saskia Coulson, Mel Woods, Michelle Scott, Drew Hemment, and Mara Balestrini. 2018. Stop the noise! Enhancing meaningfulness in participatory sensing with community level indicators. In *Proceedings of the 2018 Designing Interactive Systems Conference (DIS '18)*. ACM, New York, NY, pp. 1183–1192. DOI: 10.1145/3196709.3196762. 71

Michela Cozza and Antonella De Angeli. 2015. Infrastructuring diversity in stereotypes. *Proceeding of the 5th International Workshop on Infrastructures for Healthcare (IHC): Patient-centered Care and Patient-generated Data*. 45

Peter Dalsgaard. 2010. Challenges of participation in large-scale public projects. In *Proceedings of the 11th Biennial Participatory Design Conference (PDC '10)*. ACM, New York, NY, pp. 21–30. DOI: 10.1145/1900441.1900445. 45

Rogério DePaula. 2004. Lost in translation: a critical analysis of actors, artifacts, agendas, and arenas in participatory design. In *Proceedings of the Eighth Conference on Participatory design: Artful Integration: Interweaving Media, Materials and Practices* 1. ACM, New York, NY, pp. 162–172. DOI: 10.1145/1011870.1011890. 109

Christian Dindler and Ole S. Iversen. 2014. Relational expertise in participatory design. In *Proceedings of the 13th Participatory Design Conference: Research Papers* 1 (PDC '14), pp. 41–50. DOI: 10.1145/2661435.2661452. xviii, 61, 109

Christian Dindler and Ole Sejer Iversen. 2007. Fictional inquiry—design collaboration in a shared narrative space, *CoDesign* 3(4): pp. 213–234, DOI: 10.1080/15710880701500187. 45, 54

Christian Dindler, Eva Eriksson, Ole Sejer Iversen, Andreas Lykke-Olesen, and Martin Ludvigsen. 2005. Mission from Mars: a method for exploring user requirements for children in a narrative space. In *Proceedings of the 2005 Conference on Interaction Design and Children (IDC '05)*. ACM, New York, NY, pp. 40–47. DOI: h10.1145/1109540.1109546. 68, 73, 114

Christian Dindler, Ole Sejer Iversen, Michael E. Caspersen, and Rachel Charlotte Smith. 2021. Computational empowerment. *Computational Thinking Education in K-12: Artificial Intelligence Literacy and Physical Computing*, Siu-Cheung Kong and Hsrold Abelson, Eds., MIT Press. 39

Dindler, C., Rachel Smith, and Ole Sejer Iversen. 2020. Computational empowerment: participatory design in education. *CoDesign* 16(1): pp. 66-80. DOI: 10.1080/15710882.2020.1722173.

Christian Dindler, Ole Sejer Iversen, Rachel Smith, and Rune Veerasawmy. 2010. Participatory design at the museum: inquiring into children's everyday engagement in cultural heritage. In *Proceedings of the 22nd Conference of the Computer-Human Interaction Special Interest*

*Group of Australia on Computer-Human Interaction (OZCHI '10)*. ACM, New York, NY, pp. 72–79. DOI: 10.1145/1952222.1952239. 54

Betsy DiSalvo, Jason Yip, Elizabeth Bonsignore, and Carl DiSalvo. 2017. *Participatory Design for Learning Perspectives from Practice and Research*, Routledge. DOI: 10.4324/9781315630830. 114

Allison Druin. 1999. Cooperative inquiry: developing new technologies for children with children. In *Proceedings of the SIGCHI Conference on Human Factors in Computing Systems (CHI '99)*. ACM, New York, NY, pp. 592–599. DOI: 10.1145/302979.303166. 37, 45

Pelle Ehn and Dan Sjögren. 1991. From system descriptions to scripts for action. *Design at Work: Cooperative Design of Computer Systems*. L. Erlbaum Associates Inc., pp. 241–268. DOI: 10.1201/9781003063988-14. 54

Pelle Ehn and Morten Kyng. 1987. The collective resource approach to systems design. In *Computers and Democracy – A Scandinavian Challenge*. G. Bjerknes, P. Ehn, and M. Kyng, Eds., Gower Publishing Ltd, pp. 17–58. 9, 28

Pelle Ehn and Morten Kyng. 1991. Cardboard computers: Mocking-it-up or hands-on the future. In *Design at Work*, J. Greenbaum and M. Kyng, Eds., L. Erlbaum Associates Inc., Hillsdale, NJ, pp. 169–196. DOI: 10.1201/9781003063988-11. 12, 17, 57, 66

Pelle Ehn and Morten Kyng. 1984. A tool perspective on design of interactive computer support for skilled workers. In Saaksjarvi, Ed., *Report of the Seventh Scandinavian Research Seminar on Systemeering Helsinki School of Economics*, Studies B-74, Helsinki, pp. 211–242. 76

Pelle Ehn and Åke Sandberg. 1979. *Företagsstyrning och Löntagarmakt*. Prisma. 9, 17

Pelle Ehn and Åke Sandberg. 1983. Local union influence on technology and work organization — Some results from the demos project. In *Proceedings of the IFIP WG 9.1 Working Conference on Systems Design For, With, and by the Users*, Riva Del Sole, Italy, pp. 20–24 September 1982. North-Holland, pp. 427–437. Retrieved from: https://books.google.dk/books?id=72NPAAAAMAAJ. 17

Pelle Ehn, Elisabet M. Nilsson, and Richard Topgaard. 2014. *Making Futures—Marginal Notes on Innovation, Design and Democracy*. MIT Press. DOI: 10.7551/mitpress/9874.001.0001. 61, 97

Pelle Ehn. 1988. Work-oriented design of computer artifacts. *Falköping*: Almqvist and Wiksell International. 10, 28, 96

Pelle Ehn. 1989. The art and science of designing computer artifacts. *Scandinavian Journal of Information Systems* 1: pp. 21–42. 80

Pelle Ehn. 2014. Utopias lost and futures-in-the-making: Marginal notes on innovation, design and democracy. In *Proceedings of the 13th Participatory Design Conference: Short Papers, Industry Cases, Workshop Descriptions, Doctoral Consortium Papers, and Keynote Abstracts*, Volume 2 (PDC'14). ACM, New York, NY, pp. 191–193. DOI: 10.1145/2662155.2662214. 17, 19

Henrik Enquist, Konrad Tollmar, and Aino Vonge Corry. 2007. Interaction Ecologies Workshop paper, *Pervasive Computing*. 32, 45

Christiane Floyd, Fanny-Michaela Reisin, and Gerhard Schmidt. 1989. STEPS to software development with users. *2nd European Software Engineering Conference*, University of Warwick, Coventry, UK, September 11–15, 1989, Proceedings, Springer LNCS 387, pp. 48–64. 77, 82

Christiane Floyd. 1984. A systematic look at prototyping. In *Approaches to Prototyping*, R. Budde, K. Kuhlenkamp, L. Mathiassen, and H. Zullighoven, Eds. Springer-Verlag New York, Inc. 56

Christiane Floyd. 1987. Outline of a paradigm change in software engineering. In G. Bjerknes, P. Ehn, and M. Kyng, Eds., *Computers and Democracy—a Scandinavian Challenge*. Dower Publishing Company, Aldershot, Hampshire, pp. 192–210. 7, 12, 28, 56

Asbjørn Ammitzbøll Flügge, Thomas Hildebrandt, and Naja Holten Møller. 2021. Street-level algorithms and ai in bureaucratic decision-making: a caseworker perspective. *Proceedngs ACM Human-Computer Interactions 5*, CSCW1, Article 40 (April 2021), 23 pages. DOI: 10.1145/3449114.

Gerhard Fischer and Andreas C. Lemke. 1987. Construction kits and design environments: steps toward human problem-domain communication, *Human–Computer Interaction* 3(3): pp. 179–222, DOI: 10.1207/s15327051hci0303_1. 61

Christopher Frauenberger, Judith Good, Geraldine Fitzpatrick, and Ole Sejer Iversen. 2015. In pursuit of rigor and accountability in participatory design. *International Journal of Human-Computer Studies* 74, Elsevier, pp. 93–106. DOI: 10.1016/j.ijhcs.2014.09.004. xviii, 38, 62, 87, 88, 89, 90

Paulo Freire. 1970. *Pedagogy of the Oppressed*. Bloomsbury Publishing. 10

Batya Friedman, David G. Hendry, and Alan Borning. 2017. A survey of value sensitive design methods. *Foundations and Trends in Human–Computer Interaction* 11(2): pp. 63–125. DOI: 10.1561/1100000015. ISSN 1551–3955. 21

Julia A. Garde and Mascha C. van der Voort. 2014. Participants' view on personal gains and PD process, In *Proceedings of the 13th Participatory Design Conference: Short Papers, Industry*

*Cases, Workshop Descriptions, Doctoral Consortium Papers, and Keynote Abstracts (PDC '14),* pp. 79–82, DOI: 10.1145/2662155.2662194. 98, 101

Johannes Gärtner and Ina Wagner. 1996. Mapping actors and agendas: political frameworks of systems design and participation. *Human–Computer Interaction* 11(3): pp. 187-214. DOI: 10.1207/s15327051hci1103_1. 109

Bill Gaver, Tony Dunne, and Elena Pacenti. 1999. Design: cultural probes. *Interactions*, 6(1), pp. 21–29. ACM. DOI: 10.1145/291224.291235. 73

Chiara Del Gaudio, Leonardo Parra-Agudelo, Rachel Clarke, Joanna Saad-Sulonen, Andrea Botero, Felipe César Londoño, and Paula Escandón. 2020. *PDC '20: Proceedings of the 16th Participatory Design Conference 2020 - Participation(s) Otherwise* 1, Manizales, Colombia, ACM, New York, NY. DOI: 10.1145/3385010. 112, 113

Aakash Gautam, Chandani Shrestha, Andrew Kulak, Steve Harrison, and Deborah Tatar. 2018. Participatory tensions in working with a vulnerable population. In *Proceedings of the 15th Participatory Design Conference: Short Papers, Situated Actions, Workshops and Tutorial* 2. ACM, New York, NY, Article 26, pp. 1–5. DOI: 10.1145/3210604.3210629. 91

Alix Gerber. 2018. Participatory speculation: futures of public safety. In *Proceedings of the 15th Participatory Design Conference: Short Papers, Situated Actions, Workshops and Tutorial* 2. ACM, New York, NY, Article 23, pp. 1–4. DOI: 10.1145/3210604.3210640. 56, 73

Victoria Gerrard and Ricardo Sosa. 2014. Examining participation. In *Proceedings of the 13th Participatory Design Conference: Research Papers* 1 *(PDC '14),* pp. 111–120. DOI: 10.1145/2661435.2661451. 101

Sucheta Ghoshal and Amy Bruckman. 2019. The role of social computing technologies in grassroots movement building. *ACM Transactions Computer-Human Interactions* 26(3), Article 18 (June 2019), 36 pages. DOI: 10.1145/3318140. 10

Kaj Grønbæk, Jonathan Grudin, Susanne Bødker, and Liam Bannon. 2017. Achieving cooperative system design : Shifting from a product to a process focus. *Participatory Design: Principles and Practices.* CRC Press, pp. 79–97. DOI: 10.1201/9780203744338-5. 7

Kaj Grønbæk and Preben H. Mogensen. 1997. Informing general CSCW product development through cooperative design in specific work domains. *Computer Supported Cooperative Work (CSCW)* 6(4): pp. 275–304. DOI: 10.1023/A:1008626106968. 68

Kaj Grønbæk, Morten Kyng, and Preben Mogensen. 1993. CSCW challenges: cooperative design in engineering projects. *Communications of the ACM* 36(6): pp. 67–77. DOI: 10.1145/153571.163272. 68, 77, 82

Erik Grönvall and Morten Kyng. 2011. Beyond Utopia: reflections on participatory design in home-based healthcare with weak users. In *Proceedings of the 29th Annual European Conference on Cognitive Ergonomics (ECCE '11)*. ACM, New York, NY, pp. 189–196. DOI: 10.1145/2074712.2074750. 32, 45

Mona Leigh Guha, Allison Druin, Gene Chipman, Jerry Alan Fails, Sante Simms, and Allison Farber. 2004. Mixing ideas: a new technique for working with young children as design partners. In *Proceedings of the 2004 Conference on Interaction Design and Children: Building a Community, (IDC '04)*, pp. 35–42. 56

Wendy Gunn, Ton Otto, and Rachel Charlotte Smith, Eds. 2013. *Design Anthropology: Theory and Practice. London.* Bloomsbury Academic. 51

Joan Greenbaum and Morten Kyng. 1991. *Design at Work: Cooperative Design of Computer Systems.* Erlbaum. DOI: 10.1080/01449299208924335. 13, 28, 51, 64, 66, 67

Kim Halskov and Peter Dalsgaard. 2006. Inspiration card workshops. In *Proceedings of the 6th Conference on Designing Interactive Systems (DIS '06)*, pp. 2–11. DOI: 10.1145/1142405.1142409. 54

Kim Halskov and Peter Dalsgaard. 2007. The emergence of ideas: The interplay between sources of inspiration and emerging design concepts. *Journal of CoDesign* 3(4): pp. 185–211. DOI: 10.1080/15710880701607404. 54

Nicolai Brodersen Hansen. 2017. Materials in participatory design processes. arXiv.org 1703.07187. Ph.D. thesis. 74

Nicolai Brodersen Hansen, Christian Dindler, Kim Halskov, Ole Sejer Iversen, Claus Bossen, Ditte Amund Basballe, and Ben Schouten. 2019. How participatory design works: mechanisms and effects. In *Proceedings of the 31st Australian Conference on Human-Computer-Interaction (OZCHI'19)*. ACM, New York, NY, pp. 30–41. DOI: 10.1145/3369457.3369460. xviii, 50, 89, 97

Dean M. G. Hargreaves and Toni Robertson. 2012. Remote participatory prototyping enabled by emerging social technologies. In *Proceedings of the 12th Participatory Design Conference: Exploratory Papers, Workshop Descriptions, Industry Cases* 2: pp. 25–28. DOI: 10.1145/2348144.2348153. 57

Morten Hertzum and Jesper Simonsen. 2010. Effects-driven IT development: an instrument for supporting sustained participatory design. In *Proceedings of the 11th Biennial Participatory Design Conference (PDC '10)*, pp. 61–70. DOI: 10.1145/1900441.1900451. 32, 45, 57, 100

Karen Holtzblatt and Hugh Beyer. 1997. *Contextual Design: Defining Customer-Centered Systems (Interactive Technologies)*. 1st edition, Morgan Kaufmann. DOI: 10.1145/286498.286629. 10, 21, 51, 76

Rudy A. Hirschheim. 1983. Assessing participative systems design: Some conclusions from an exploratory study. *Information and Management* 6(6): pp. 317–327, DOI:10.1016/0378-7206(83)90040-X. 101

Liesbeth Huybrechts and Maurizio Teli, Eds. 2020. The politics of co-design, *CoDesign*, 16(1). DOI: 10.1080/15710882.2020.1728150. 112

Liesbeth Huybrechts, Maurizio Teli, Ann Light, Yanki Lee, Julie Garde, John Vines, Eva Brandt, Anne Marie Kanstrup, and Keld Bødker, Eds. 2018. PDC 2018 participatory design, democracy and politics. *Proceedings of the 15th Participatory Design Conference Volume I: Full Papers. 15th Participatory Design Conference*. ACM. DOI: 10.1145/3210604. 112

Sofia Hussain and Elizabeth B.-N. Sanders. 2012. Fusion of horizons: Co-designing with Cambodian children who have prosthetic legs, using generative design tools, *CoDesign* 8(1): pp. 43–79, DOI: 10.1080/15710882.2011.637113. 73

Hilary Hutchinson, Wendy Mackay, Bo Westerlund, Benjamin B. Bederson, Allison Druin, Catherine Plaisant, Michel Beaudouin-Lafon, Stéphane Conversy, Helen Evans, Heiko Hansen, Nicolas Roussel, and Björn Eiderbäck. 2003. Technology probes: inspiring design for and with families. In *Proceedings of the SIGCHI Conference on Human Factors in Computing Systems (CHI '03)*. ACM, New York, NY, pp. 17–24. DOI: 10.1145/642611.642616. 67

Minna Isomursu, Kari Kuutti, and Soili Vainamo. 2004. Experience clip: method for user participation and evaluation of mobile concepts. In *Proceedings of the Eighth Conference on Participatory Design: Artful Integration: Interweaving Media, Materials and Practices - Volume 1 (PDC '04)*, pp. 83–92. DOI: 10.1145/1011870.1011881. 72

Mimi Ito. 2009. *Hanging Out, Messing Around, and Geeking Out: Kids Living and Learning with New Media*. Cambridge, MA: MIT Press. 40

Ole Sejer Iversen and Christian Dindler. 2008. Pursuing aesthetic inquiry in participatory design. In *Proceedings of the Tenth Anniversary Conference on Participatory Design 2008 (PDC '08)*, pp. 138–145. 37, 56, 73, 105

Ole Sejer Iversen and Christian Dindler. 2014. Sustaining participatory design initiatives, *CoDesign: International Journal of CoCreation in Design and the Arts*, DOI: 10.1080/15710882.2014.963124. xviii, 60

Ole Sejer Iversen and Rachel Charlotte Smith. 2012. Scandinavian participatory design: dialogic curation with teenagers. In *Proceedings of the 11th International Conference on*

*Interaction Design and Children (IDC '12)*. ACM, New York, NY, pp. 106–115. DOI: 10.1145/2307096.2307109. 34, 39

Ole Sejer Iversen and Tuck W. Leong. 2012. Values-led participatory design: mediating the emergence of values. In *Proceedings of the 7th Nordic Conference on Human-Computer Interaction: Making Sense Through Design (NordiCHI '12)*. ACM, New York, NY, pp. 468–477. DOI: 10.1145/2399016.2399087. 88

Ole Sejer Iversen, Kim Halskov, and Tuck W. Leong. 2012. Values-led participatory design, *CoDesign* 8(2–3): pp. 87–103. DOI: 10.1080/15710882.2012.672575. 88

Ole Sejer Iversen, Kim Halskov, and Tuck Wah Leong. 2010. Rekindling values in participatory design. In *Proceedings of the 11th Biennial Participatory Design Conference (PDC '10)*. ACM, New York, NY, pp. 91–100. DOI: 10.1145/1900441.1900455. 88

Ole Sejer Iversen, Rachel Charlotte Smith, and Christian Dindler. 2018. From computational thinking to computational empowerment: a 21st century PD agenda. In *Proceedings of the 15th Participatory Design Conference: Full Papers* 1: pp. 1–11. DOI: 10.1145/3210586.3210592. 114

Ole Sejer Iversen, Rachel Charlotte Smith, and Christian Dindler. 2017. Child as protagonist: Expanding the role of children in participatory design. In *Proceedings of the 2017 Conference on Interaction Design and Children*, pp. 27–37. DOI: 10.1145/3078072.3079725. 37

Ole Sejer Iversen. 2005. *Participatory Design Beyond Work Practices: Designing with Children*. University of Aarhus. 37, 45

Michael A. Jackson. 1983. *System Development*, Prentice Hall. 21

Robert Jungk and Norbert Müllert 1987. *Future Workshops: How to Create Desirable Futures*. London, England, Institute for Social Inventions. 11, 54

Jens Kaasbøll. 1983. *The Research Program SYDPOL: SYstem Development Environment and Profession Oriented Languages (in Scandinavian)*, Nordforsk Publikationsserie 1983:2, Department of Informatics, University of Oslo. 61, 71, 114

Asnath Paula Kambunga, Heike Winschiers-Theophilus, and Rachel Charlotte Smith. 2020. Participatory memory making: Creating postcolonial dialogic engagements with namibian youth. *Proceedings of the 2020 ACM Designing Interactive Systems Conference*. New York, NY, pp. 785–797. DOI: 10.1145/3357236.3395441. 35

Gopinaath Kannabiran and Susanne Bødker. 2020. Prototypes as objects of desire. In *Proceedings of the 2020 ACM Designing Interactive Systems Conference (DIS '20)*. ACM, New York, NY, pp. 1619–1631. DOI: 10.1145/3357236.3395487. 57

Anne Marie Kanstrup and Pernille Bertelsen. 2016. Bringing new voices to design of exercise technology: participatory design with vulnerable young adults. In *Proceedings of the 14th Participatory Design Conference: Full Papers - Volume 1 (PDC '16)*, pp. 121–130. DOI: 10.1145/2940299.2940305. 56, 91

Anne Marie Kanstrup, Pernille Bertelsen, and Jacob Ø. Madsen. 2014. Design with the feet: walking methods and participatory design. In *Proceedings of the 13th Participatory Design Conference: Research Papers - Volume 1 (PDC '14)*, pp. 51–60. DOI: 10.1145/2661435.2661441.

Victor Kaptelinin and Liam J. Bannon. 2012. Interaction design beyond the product: Creating technology-enhanced activity spaces. *Human Computer Interaction* 27(3): pp. 277–309. 61, 108

Gereon Koch Kapuire, Heike Winschiers-Theophilus, and Edwin Blake. 2015. An insider perspective on community gains: a subjective account of a Namibian rural communities' perception of a long-term participatory design project. *International Journal of Human Computer Studies* 74: pp. 124–143. DOI:10.1016/j.ijhcs.2014.10.004. 35, 101

Helena Karasti. 2014. Infrastructuring in participatory design. In *Proceedings of the 13th Participatory Design Conference: Research Papers - Volume 1 (PDC '14)*, pp. 141–150. DOI: 10.1145/2661435.2661450. 60

Karl Kautz. 2010. Inclusive design in practice: A study of participatory design, customer and user involvement in agile software development. In J. Molka-Danielsen, Ed., *Proceedings of the 32nd Information Systems Research Seminar in Scandinavia*, IRIS 32, Inclusive Design, Molde University College, Molde, Norway, August 9–12, pp. 217–230. 77

Rebecca Kelly, Emanuela Mazzone, Matthew Horton, and Janet C. Read. 2006. Bluebells: a design method for child-centered product development. In *Proceedings of the 4th Nordic Conference on Human-Computer Interaction: Changing Roles (NordiCHI '06)*. ACM, New York, NY, pp. 361–368. DOI: 10.1145/1182475.1182513. 37, 45

Finn Kensing and Joan Greenbaum. 2013. Heritage: Having a say. In *Routledge International Handbook of Participatory Design*, pp. 21–36. Routledge. 76, 85, 91

Finn Kensing and Kim Halskov Madsen. 1991. Generating visions: Future workshops and metaphors. In *Design at Work: Cooperative Design of Computer Systems*, J. Greenbaum and M. Kyng, Eds. L. Erlbaum Assoc. Inc., Hillsdale, NJ., pp. 155–168. DOI: 10.1201/9781003063988-10. 54

Finn Kensing, Jesper Simonsen, and Keld Bødker. 1996. MUST—a method for participatory design, In *Proceedings of the Fourth Biennial Conference on Participatory Design (PDC '96)*, pp. 129–140. 62, 76, 82

Julia Klammer, Fred van den Anker, and Monique Janneck. 2010. Embedding participatory design processes into everyday work activities: the case of video consultation services for paraplegics. In *Proceedings of the 11th Biennial Participatory Design Conference (PDC '10)*. ACM, New York, NY, pp. 219–222. DOI: 10.1145/1900441.1900485. 32, 45

Eva Knutz, Tau Ulv Lenskjold, and Thomas Markussen. 2016. Fiction as a resource in participatory design. In: *Proceedings of DRS 2016 International Conference: Future–Focused Thinking*. Design Research Society, pp. 1830–1844. DOI: 10.21606/drs.2016.476. 73

Matthias Korn and Pär-Ola Zander. 2010. From workshops to walkshops: Evaluating mobile location-based applications in realistic settings. *Proceedings of OMUE Workshop at NordiCHI* 10: pp. 29–32. 42, 56

Matthias Korn and Susanne Bødker. 2012. Looking ahead: How field trials can work in iterative and exploratory design of ubicomp systems. *Proceedings of the 2012 ACM Conference on Ubiquitous Computing*. ACM, New York, pp. 21–30. DOI: 10.1145/2370216.2370221. 42

Morten Kyng. 1994. From subversion to hype: On political and technical agendas in PD. *Proceedings of PDC 94*, 1. Palo Alto, CA: CPSR. 86

Morten Kyng and Lars Mathiassen. 1980. Systems development and trade union activities. *DAIMI Report Series* 8, 99 (1980). DOI: 10.7146/dpb.v8i99.6515. 17

Morten Kyng and Lars Mathiassen. 1982. Systems development and trade union activities. *Information Society, For Richer, For Poorer*, N. Bjørn-Andersen, Ed., Amsterdam: North-Holland, pp. 247–60. 17

Morten Kyng and Lars Mathiassen. 1997. *Computers and Design in Context*. MIT Press. 28

Morten Kyng, Esben Toftdahl Nielsen, and Margit Kristensen. 2006. Challenges in designing interactive systems for emergency response. In *Proceedings of the 6th Conference on Designing Interactive Systems (DIS '06)*. ACM, New York, NY, pp. 301–310. DOI: 10.1145/1142405.1142450. 32, 45

Morten Kyng. 1995. Making representations work. *Communications of the ACM* 38(9): pp. 46–55. DOI: 10.1145/223248.223261. 78, 79

Morten Kyng. 2015. On creating and sustaining alternatives: the case of Danish telehealth. In *Proceedings of The Fifth Decennial Aarhus Conference on Critical Alternatives (AA '15)*. Aarhus University Press. pp. 5–16. DOI: 10.7146/aahcc.v1i1.21297. 33, 34, 61, 105, 107

Giovan Francesco Lanzara. 2009. Introduction in bricolage, care and information: Claudio Ciborra's legacy in information systems research. In *Technology, Work and Globalization*, C. Avgerou, G. Lanzara, and L. Willcocks, Eds., Springer. 27

Jean Lave and Etienne Wenger. 1991. *Situated Learning. Legitimate Peripheral Participation*. Cambridge: University of Cambridge Press. DOI: 10.1017/CBO9780511815355. 21

Christopher Le Dantec and Carl DiSalvo. 2013. Infrastructuring and the formation of publics in participatory design. *Social Studies of Science* 42(2): pp. 241–264. DOI: 10.1177/0306312712471581. 43, 45

Christopher Le Dantec. 2012. Participation and publics: supporting community engagement. In *Proceedings of the SIGCHI Conference on Human Factors in Computing Systems (CHI '12)*. ACM, New York, NY, pp. 1351–1360. DOI: 10.1145/2207676.2208593.

Tuck W. Leong and Ole S. Iversen. 2015. Values-led Participatory Design as a Pursuit of Meaningful Alternatives. In *Proceedings of the Annual Meeting of the Australian Special Interest Group for Computer Human Interaction (OzCHI '15)*, pp. 314–323. DOI: 10.1145/2838739.2838784. 56

Ann Light and Yoko Akama. 2012. The human touch: participatory practice and the role of facilitation in designing with communities. In *Proceedings of the 12th Participatory Design Conference: Research Papers - Volume 1 (PDC '12)*. ACM, New York, NY, pp. 61–70. DOI: 10.1145/2347635.2347645. 109

Susanne Lindberg, Michel Thomsen, and Maria Åkesson. 2014. Ethics in health promoting PD: designing digital peer support with children cured from cancer. In *Proceedings of the 13th Participatory Design Conference: Research Papers - Volume 1 (PDC '14)*, pp. 91–100. DOI: 10.1145/2661435.2661449. 56

Signe Lindquist, Bo Westerlund, Yngve Sundblad, Helena Tobiasson, Michel Beaudouin-Lafon, and Wendy Mackay. 2007. Co-designing communication technology with and for families – methods, experience, results and impact. In N. Streitz, A. Kameas, and I. Mavrommati, Eds., *The Disappearing Computer. Lecture Notes in Computer Science*, 4500. Springer, Berlin, Heidelberg. DOI: 10.1007/978-3-540-72727-9_5.

Thomas Lodato and Carl DiSalvo. 2018. Institutional constraints: the forms and limits of participatory design in the public realm. In *Proceedings of the 15th Participatory Design Conference: Full Papers - Volume 1 (PDC '18)*. ACM, New York, NY, Article 5, pp. 1–12. DOI: 10.1145/3210586.3210595. 71

Daria Loi, Thomas Lodato, Christine T. Wolf, Raphael Arar, and Jeanette Blomberg. 2018. 'PD Manifesto for AI futures'. In *Proceedings of the 15th Participatory Design Conference on Short Papers, Situated Actions, Workshops and Tutorial - PDC '18*, 1–4. Hasselt and Genk, Belgium: ACM Press. DOI: 10.1145/3210604.3210614. 115

Rachael Luck. 2018. What is it that makes participation in design participatory design? *Design Studies* 59: pp. 1–8. DOI: 10.1016/j.destud.2018.10.002. 91

Peter Lyle, Mariacristina Sciannamblo, and Maurizio Teli. 2017. Fostering commonfare. strategies and tactics in a collaborative project. In *Proceedings of the 29th Australian Conference on Computer-Human Interaction (OZCHI '17)*. ACM, New York, NY, pp. 443–447. DOI: 10.1145/3152771.3156154. 24, 26

Wendy E. Mackay, D. S. Pagani, L. Faber, B. Inwood, P. Launiainen, L. Brenta, and V. Pouzol. 1995. Ariel: augmenting paper engineering drawings. In *Conference Companion on Human Factors in Computing Systems (CHI '95)*. ACM, New York, NY, pp. 421–422. DOI: 10.1145/223355.223763. 68

Henry Mainsah and Andrew Morrison. 2014. Participatory design through a cultural lens: insights from postcolonial theory. In *Proceedings of the 13th Participatory Design Conference - PDC '14* 2: pp. 83–86. DOI: 10.1145/2662155.2662195. 29

Julia Makhaeva, Christopher Frauenberger, and Katharina Spiel. 2016. Creating creative spaces for co-designing with autistic children: the concept of a "Handlungsspielraum". In *Proceedings of the 14th Participatory Design Conference: Full papers - Volume 1 (PDC '16)*, pp. 51–60. DOI: 10.1145/2940299.2940306. 38, 56

Peter Mambrey, Gloria Mark, and Uta Pankoke-Babatz. 1996. Integrating user advocacy into participatory design: The designers' perspective. In *Proceedings of PDC 1996*, CSCPR, pp. 251–259.

Bruno Marques, Greg Grabasch, and Jacqueline McIntosh. 2021. Fostering landscape identity through participatory design with indigenous cultures of Australia and Aotearoa/New Zealand. *Space and Culture* 24(1):pp. 37–52. DOI: 10.1177/1206331218783939.

Sanna Marttila, Andrea Botero, and Joanna Saad-Sulonen. 2014. Toward commons design in participatory design. In *Proceedings of the 13th Participatory Design Conference: Short Papers, Industry Cases, Workshop Descriptions, Doctoral Consortium papers, and Keynote abstracts - Volume 2 (PDC '14)*. ACM, New York, NY, pp. 9–12. DOI: 10.1145/2662155.2662187. 113

Tuuli Mattelmäki. 2008. Probing for co-exploring. *CoDesign* 4(1): pp. 65–78, DOI: 10.1080/15710880701875027. 73

Cecelia B. Merkel, Lu Xiao, Umer Farooq, Craig H. Ganoe, Roderick Lee, John M. Carroll, and Mary B. Rosson. 2004. Participatory design in community computing contexts: tales from the field. In *Proceedings of the Eighth Conference on Participatory Design: Artful Inte-*

*gration: Interweaving Media, Materials and Practices - Volume 1 (PDC 04)*, pp. 1–10. DOI: 10.1145/1011870.1011872. 62, 101, 108

Preben Mogensen and Randy H. Trigg. 1992. Artifacts as triggers for participatory analysis. *PDC'92.* pp. 55–62. DOI: 10.7146/dpb.v21i413.6726. 54

Preben Mogensen. 1992. Toward a provotyping approach in systems development, *Scandinavian Journal of Information Systems* 4(1), Article 5. Available at: https://aisel.aisnet.org/sjis/vol4/iss1/5. 57, 68

Andreas Munk-Madsen and Finn Kensing. 1993. Participatory design: Structure in the toolbox, *CACM* 36(4). DOI: 10.1145/153571.163278. 64

Anders I. Mørch, Gunnar Stevens, Markus Won, Markus Klann, Yvonne Dittrich, and Volker Wulf. 2004. Component-based technologies for end-user development. *Communications* 47(9): pp. 59–62. DOI: 10.1145/1015864.1015890. 61

Anders Mørch. 1997. Three levels of end-user tailoring: Customization, integration, and extension. In *Computers and Design in Context*, 1997. 61

Gareth Morgan. 1986. *Images of Organization*, Sage Publications (originally published in 1986). 6

Michael J. Muller and Allison Druin. 2012. Participatory design, the third space in human–computer interaction. In *The Human–Computer Interaction Handbook*, 3rd ed. CRC Press, p. 29. DOI: 10.1201/b11963-57. 64

Michael J. Muller and Sarah Kuhn. 1993. Participatory design. *Communictions of the ACM* 36(6): pp. 24-28. DOI: 10.1145/153571.255960. 63

Enid Mumford. 1997. The reality of participative systems design: contributing to stability in a rocking boat. *Information Systems Journal* 7(4): pp. 309–322. DOI: 10.1046/j.1365-2575.1997.00020.x. 2

Larissa Vivian Nägele, Merja Ryöppy, and Danielle Wilde. 2018. PDFi: participatory design fiction with vulnerable users. In *Proceedings of the 10th Nordic Conference on Human-Computer Interaction (NordiCHI '18)*. ACM, New York, NY, pp. 819–831. DOI: 10.1145/3240167.3240272. 56, 73

Kristen Nygaard and Olav-Terje Bergo. 1975. The trade unions-New users of research. *Personnel Review* 4(2): pp. 5–10. DOI: 10.1108/eb055278. 9, 11, 17, 18, 19, 96, 114

Hartmut Obendorf, Monique Janneck, and Matthias Finck. 2009. Inter-contextual distributed participatory design. *Scandinavian Journal of Information Systems* 21(1) Article 2. Available at: https://aisel.aisnet.org/sjis/vol21/iss1/2. 78, 106

Tom C. Pape and Kari Thoresen Pape. 1987. Development of common. Systems by prototyping. In G. Bjerknes, P. Ehn, and, M. Kyng, Eds., *Computers and Democracy,* Erlbaum. 76

Sofie Pilemalm. 2018. Adapting participatory design to emerging civic engagement initiatives in *the new public sector: Renewing PD concepts in resource-scarce organizations. ACM Transactions on Computer-Human Interaction* 25(1): pp. 1–26. DOI: 10.1145/3152420. 40, 45

Volkmar Pipek and Helge Kahler. 2006. Supporting collaborative tailoring. In *End User Development. Human-Computer Interaction Series,* H. Lieberman, F. Paternò, and V. Wulf, Eds., 9. Springer, Dordrecht. DOI: 10.1007/1-4020-5386-X_15. 61

Volkmar Pipek and Volker Wulf. 2009. Infrastructuring: Toward an integrated perspective on the design and use of information technology. *Journal of the Association for Information Systems* 10(5): pp. 447–473. DOI: 10.17705/1jais.00195. 7

Giacomo Poderi and Yvonne Dittrich. 2018. Participatory design and sustainability: a literature review of PDC proceedings. In *Proceedings of the 15th Participatory Design Conference: Short Papers, Situated Actions, Workshops and Tutorial - Volume 2 (PDC '18).* ACM, New York, NY, Article 2, pp. 1–5. DOI: 10.1145/3210604.3210624. 104

Jennifer Preece, Helen Sharp, and Yvonne Rogers. 2019. *Interaction Design: Beyond Human-Computer Interaction,* 5th edition. John Wiley and Sons. 1, 50, 77, 99

Marc Prensky. 2001. Digital natives, digital immigrants. In *On the Horizon,* MCB University Press, 9(5). DOI: 10.1108/10748120110424816. 40

Janet C. Read, Peggy Gregory, Stuart MacFarlane, Barbara McManus, Peter Gray, and Raj Patel. 2002. An investigation of participatory design with children-informant, balanced and facilitated design. In *Interaction Design and Children,* Eindhoven, pp. 53–64. 37, 45

Janet C. Read, Daniel Fitton, Gavin Sim, and Matt Horton. 2016. How ideas make it through to designs: Process and practice. In *Proceedings of the 9th Nordic Conference on Human-Computer Interaction (NordiCHI '16).* ACM, New York, NY, Article 16, pp. 1–10. DOI: 10.1145/2971485.2971560. 37

Christine Reidl, Marianne Tolar, and Ina Wagner. 2008. Impediments to change: the case of implementing an electronic patient record in three oncology clinics. In *Proceedings of the Tenth Anniversary Conference on Participatory Design 2008 (PDC '08).* Indiana University, pp. 21–30. 32, 45

Toni Robertson, Tuck W. Leong, Jeannette Durick, and Treffyn Koreshoff. 2014. Mutual learning as a resource for research design. *Proceedings of the 13th Participatory Design Conference on Short Papers, Industry Cases, Workshop Descriptions, Doctoral Consortium Papers, and Keynote Abstracts - PDC '14* 2. DOI: 10.1145/2662155.2662181.

Mike Robinson. 1991. Double-level languages and co-operative working. *AI and Society* 5: pp. 34–60. DOI: 10.1007/BF01891356. 42

Kasper Rodil, Heike Winschiers-Theophilus, Kasper Jensen, and Matthias Rehm 2012. Homestead creator: A tool for indigenous designers. In *Proceedings of the 7th Nordic Conference on Human-Computer Interaction: Making Sense Through Design*, ACM, pp. 627–630. DOI: 10.1145/2399016.2399111. 36

Winston W. Royce. 1987 [original 1970]. Managing the development of large software systems: concepts and techniques. In *Proceedings of the 9th International Conference on Software Engineering.* 77

Marco C. Rozendaal, Marie L. Heidingsfelder, and Frank Kupper. 2016. Exploring embodied speculation in participatory design and innovation. In *Proceedings of the 14th Participatory Design Conference: Short Papers, Interactive Exhibitions, Workshops - Volume 2 (PDC '16).* ACM, New York, NY, pp. 100–102. DOI: 10.1145/2948076.2948102. 56, 73

Joanna Saad-Sulonen. 2014. Combining Participations. Aalto University Ph.D. thesis. 40

SAFE Expert Systems. 1987. G. Bjerknes, P. Ehn, and M. Kyng, Eds., *Computers and Democracy - a Scandinavian Challenge.* Gower Publishing, p. 419. 28

Pablo Calderon Salazar and Liesbeth Huybrechts. 2020. PD otherwise will be pluriversal (or it won't be). In *Proceedings of the 16th Participatory Design Conference 2020 - Participation(s) Otherwise - Volume 1 (PDC '20).* ACM, New York, NY, pp. 107–115. DOI: 10.1145/3385010.3385027. 29

Elizabeth B.-N. Sanders, Eva Brandt, and Thomas Binder. 2010. A framework for organizing the tools and techniques of participatory design. In *Proceedings of the 11th Biennial Participatory Design Conference (PDC '10).* ACM, New York, NY, pp. 195–198. DOI: 10.1145/1900441.1900476. 63

Elizabeth Sander and Pieter Jan Stappers. 2008. Co-creation and the new landscapes of design. *CoDesign* 4(1): pp. 5–18. DOI: 10.1080/15710880701875068. 8, 21

Mariacristina Sciannamblo, Marisa Leavitt Cohn, Peter Lyle, and Maurizio Teli. 2021. Caring and commoning as cooperative work: A case study in Europe. *PACM on Human-Computer Interaction 5, CSCW1*, Article 126 (April 2021), 26 pages. DOI: 10.1145/3449200. 113

Mariacristina Sciannamblo, Peter Lyle, and Maurizio Teli. 2018. Fostering commonfare: Entanglements between participatory design and feminism. In C. Storni, K. Leahy, M. McMahon, P. Lloyd, and E. Bohemia (Eds.), *Proceedings of DRS2018* 2: pp. 458–471. Loughborough University. DOI: 10.21606/drs.2018.557. 26, 45

Donald A. Schön. 1983. *The Reflective Practitioner: How Professionals Think in Action.* New York: Basic Books, 1983. 1

Kjeld Schmidt and Liam Bannon. 1992. Taking CSCW seriously. *Journal Computer Supported Cooperative Work (CSCW)* 1(1), pp. 7–40. DOI: 10.1007/BF00752449. 76

Douglas Schuler and Aki Namioka, Eds. 1993. *Participatory Design: Perspectives on Systems Design,* Hillsdale, NJ: Lawrence Erlbaum Associates, pp. 123–155. xvi, 64

Ben Shneiderman and Catherine Plaisant. 2005. *Designing the User Interface: Strategies for Effective Human-Computer Interaction,* 4th ed. 1

Nina Simon. 2010. The participatory museum, *Museum* 2.0. 34

Jesper Simonsen and Morten Hertzum. 2008. Participative design and the challenges of large-scale systems: extending the iterative PD approach. *PDC 2008*, pp. 1–10. 101

Jesper Simonsen,and Morten Hertzum. 2012. Sustained participatory design: Extending the iterative approach. *Design Issues* 28(3). MIT Press. DOI: 10.1162/DESI_a_00158. 101

Jesper Simonsen and Toni Robertson. 2012. *Routledge International Handbook of Participatory Design.* Routledge. DOI: 10.4324/9780203108543. xvi, xviii, 1, 2, 13, 23, 28, 64, 96

Rachel Charlotte Smith and Mette Gislev Kjærsgaard. 2015. Design anthropology in participatory design. *Interaction Design and Architecture(s) Journal-IxD&A* 26: pp. 73–80. 51

Rachel Charlotte Smith and Ole Sejer Iversen. 2011. When the museum goes native. *Interactions* 18(5): pp. 15–19. DOI: 10.1145/2008176.2008182. 39, 58

Rachel Charlotte Smith and Ole Sejer Iversen. 2014. Participatory heritage innovation: designing dialogic sites of engagement, *Journal of Digital Creativity* 25(3): pp. 255–268, DOI: 10.1080/14626268.2014.904796. 34, 39

Rachel Charlotte Smith and Ole Sejer Iversen. 2018. Participatory design for sustainable social change, *Design Studies* 59: pp. 9–36, DOI: 10.1016/j.destud.2018.05.005. xviii, 38, 39, 86, 107

Rachel Charlotte Smith, Claus Bossen, and Anne Marie Kanstrup. 2017. Participatory design in an era of participation, *CoDesign* 13(2): pp. 65–69. DOI: 10.1080/15710882.2017.1310466. 24, 29, 112

Rachel Charlotte Smith, Claus Bossen, Christian Dindler, and Ole Sejer Iversen. 2020b. When participatory design becomes policy: technology comprehension in Danish education. In *Proceedings of the 16th Participatory Design Conference 2020-Participation (s) Otherwise* 1, pp. 148–158. DOI: 10.1145/3385010.3385011. 39

Rachel Charlotte Smith, Heike Winschiers-Theophilus, Asnath Paula Kambunga, and Sarala Krishnamurthy. 2020a. Decolonising participatory design: Memory making in Namibia. *Participatory Design Conference 2020 - Participation(s) Otherwise* 1. DOI: 10.1145/3385010.3385021. 34, 113

Rachel Charlotte Smith, Heike Winschiers-Theophilus, Daria Loi, Rogério Abreu de Paula, Asnath Paula Kambunga, Marly Muudeni Samuel, and Tariq Zaman. 2021. Decolonizing design practices: Toward pluriversality. *Extended Abstracts of the 2021 CHI Conference on Human Factors in Computing Systems*. ACM, New York, NY, Article 83, pp. 1–5. DOI: 10.1145/3411763.3441334. 25, 29, 113

Rachel Charlotte Smith, Kasper Tang Vangkilde, Ton Otto, Mette Gislev Kjærsgaard, Joachim Halse, and Thomas Binder, Eds. 2016. *Design Anthropological Futures*. Bloomsbury Publishing. 51, 52

Rachel Charlotte Smith, Ole Sejer Iversen, and Mikkel Hjorth. 2015. Design thinking for digital fabrication in education, *International Journal of Child-Computer Interaction* 5: pp. 20–28, ISSN 2212-8689, DOI: 10.1016/j.ijcci.2015.10.002. http://www.sciencedirect.com/science/article/pii/S2212868915000203. 38

Rachel Charlotte Smith. 2013. *Designing Digital Cultural Futures: Design Anthropological Sites of Transformation*, Aarhus University, Faculty of Arts, 2013. 39, 54

Ole Smørdal, Dagny Stuedahl, and Idunn Sem (2014) Experimental zones: two cases of exploring frames of participation in a dialogic museum, *Digital Creativity* 25(3): pp. 224–232, DOI: 10.1080/14626268.2014.904366.

Werner Sperschneider, Susanne Bødker, Jannie Friis Kristensen, and Christina Nielsen. 2003. Technology for boundaries. In *Proceedings of the 2003 International ACM SIG-GROUP Conference on Supporting Group Work*, Sanibel Island, FL, pp. 311–320. DOI: 10.1145/958160.958210. 40

Katta Spiel, Emeline Brulé, Christopher Frauenberger, Gilles Bailly, and Geraldine Fitzpatrick. 2018. Micro-ethics for participatory design with marginalized children. In *Proceedings of the 15th Participatory Design Conference: Full Papers - Volume 1 (PDC '18)*. ACM, New York, NY, Article 17, pp. 1–12. DOI: 10.1145/3210586.3210603. 38, 91

Colin Stanley, Heike Winschiers-Theophilus, Edwin Blake, Kasper Rodil, and Gereon Koch Kapuire. 2015. OvaHimba community in Namibia ventures into crowdsourcing design, *13th International Conference on Social Implications of Computers in Developing Countries*, pp. 20–22 May, Jetwing Blue, Negombo - Sri Lanka. 36

Bárbara Szaniecki, Bibiana Serpa, Imaíra Portela, Marina Sirito, Mariana Costard, and Sâmia Batista. 2020. Participation otherwise: Practices by/from the global south. In *Proceedings of the 16th Participatory Design Conference 2020 - Participation(s) Otherwise* 2: pp. 203–205. Manizales, Colombia: ACM. DOI: 10.1145/3384772.3385171. 25, 113

Susan Leigh Star and Karen Ruhleder. 1994. Steps toward an ecology of infrastructure: complex problems in design and access for large-scale collaborative systems. In *Proceedings of the 1994 ACM Conference on Computer Supported Cooperative Work (CSCW '94)*, pp. 253–264. DOI: 10.1145/192844.193021. 60

Lucy A. Suchman and Randall H. Trigg. 1992. Understanding practice: video as a medium for reflection and design. In *Design at Work: Cooperative Design of Computer Systems*, J. Greenbaum and M. Kyng, Eds. L. Erlbaum Associates Inc., Hillsdale, NJ, pp. 65–90. DOI: 10.1201/9781003063988-5. 51

Lucy A. Suchman. 2002. Practice-based design of information systems: notes from the hyperdeveloped world, *The Information Society* 18(2): pp. 139–144, DOI: 10.1080/01972240290075066. 109

Lucy Suchman. 1987. *Plans and Situated Actions: The Problem of Human-Machine Communication*. Cambridge University Press, New York. 21

Gustav Taxén. 2004. Introducing participatory design in museums. In *Proceedings of PDC*. ACM, New York, NY, 2004, pp. 204–213. DOI: 10.1145/1011870.1011894. 34

Philip Tchernavskij, Clemens Nylandsted Klokmose, and Michel Beaudouin-Lafon. 2017. What can software learn from hypermedia? In *Companion to the First International Conference on the Art, Science and Engineering of Programming (Programming '17)*. ACM, New York, NY, Article 29, pp. 1–5. DOI: 10.1145/3079368.3079408. 70

Pierre Tchounikine. 2016. Contribution to a theory of CSCL scripts: taking into account the appropriation of scripts by learners. *International Journal of Computer-Supported Collaborative Learning* 11(3): pp. 349–369. DOI: 10.1007/s11412-016-9240-8. 108

Maurizio Teli. 2015. Computing and the common: hints of a new utopia in participatory design. In *Proceedings of The Fifth Decennial Aarhus Conference on Critical Alternatives (CA '15)*. Aarhus University Press, Aarhus N, pp. 17–20. DOI: 10.7146/aahcc.v1i1.21318. 113

Kari Thoresen. 1990. Prototyping organizational change. In *Proceedings of the first Participatory Design Conference*. CPSR. 101

Randall H. Trigg and Susanne Bødker. 1994. From implementation to design: tailoring and the emergence of systematization in CSCW. In *Proceedings of the 1994 ACM Conference on*

*Computer Supported Cooperative Work (CSCW '94)*. ACM, New York, NY, pp. 45–54. DOI: 10.1145/192844.192869. 40, 45

Michael W. Tschudy, Elizabeth A. Dykstra-Erickson, and Matthew S. Holloway. 1996. Picture-CARD: A storytelling tool for task analysis. In *Proceedings of the 4th Biennial Participatory Design Conference (PDC'96)*. pp. 183–191. 72

Åke Walldius, Jan Gulliksen and Yngve Sundblad. 2015. Revisiting the users award program from a value sensitive design perspective. *Aarhus Series on Human Centered Computing* 1(1): p. 4. DOI: 10.7146/aahcc.v1i1.21317. 21

Greg Walsh, Allison Druin, Mona L. Guha, Elizabeth Foss, Evan Golub, Leshell Hatley, Elizabeth Bonsignore, and Sonia Franckel. 2010. Layered elaboration: a new technique for co-design with children. *Proceedings of the 28th International Conference On Human Factors In Computing Systems*, ACM (2010), pp. 1237–1240. DOI: 10.1145/1753326.1753512. 56

Heike Winschiers-Theophilus and Nicola J. Bidwell. 2013. Toward an Afro-centric indigenous HCI paradigm. *International Journal of Human-Computer Interaction* 29(4): pp. 243–255. DOI: 10.1080/10447318.2013.765763. 25, 29, 35

Heike Winschiers-Theophilus, Shilumbe Chivuno-Kuria, Gereon Koch Kapuire, Nicola J. Bidwell, and Edwin Blake. 2010. Being participated: a community approach. In *Proceedings of the 11th Biennial Participatory Design Conference on - PDC '10*, 1. DOI: 10.1145/1900441.1900443. 35

Heike Winschiers-Theophilus, Tariq Zaman, and Colin Stanley. 2017. A classification of cultural engagements in community technology design: introducing a transcultural approach. *AI and Society* 34(3): pp. 419–435. DOI: 10.1007/s00146-017-0739-y. 29, 35, 36

Jon Whittle. 2014. How much participation is enough?: A comparison of six participatory design projects in terms of outcomes. In *Proceedings of the 13th Participatory Design Conference: Research Papers - Volume 1, PDC '14*, pp. 121–130, New York, NY, 2014. ACM. DOI: 10.1145/2661435.2661445. 101

Edward Yourdon. 1994. *Object-Oriented Systems Development: An Integrated Approach*. Prentice Hall. 21

# Authors' Biographies

**Professor Susanne Bødker** has done research in Human-Computer Interaction, Computer Supported Cooperative Work, and Participatory Design since the 1980s. She was involved with starting the International Participatory Design (PDC) conference series. She does current research on how grassroot communities share technologies and on the collaboration between citizens and public organizations through technological mediation.

**Professor Ole Sejer Iversen** is director of the Center for Computational Thinking & Design at Aarhus University, Denmark. For the past seven years, he has been in the steering committee of the Participatory Design conference series and served as technical program chair of the PDC conference in 2014. During the past decades, Professor Iversen has published intensively on research related to values in Participatory Design especially with children and teens as collaborators in the design process.

**Christian Dindler** is Associate Professor of Participatory Interaction Design at Aarhus University and has worked with Participatory Design in areas such as schools and museums for more than a decade. He has published research at PDC since 2008 and taken part in organizing several PDC conferences. In his current research, he explores how Participatory Design processes unfold in industry settings and how stakeholders deal with ethical issues in design practice.

**Rachel Charlotte Smith** is Associate Professor of human-centered design at Aarhus University. Her research focuses on advancing human and participatory approaches to technology in people's everyday life, in education, cultural institutions, and industry. She is currently chair of the PDC steering committee. In 2016, she chaired the PDC conference, and has since been actively engaged in the PDC steering committee and community.

Printed in the United States
by Baker & Taylor Publisher Services